Death of an Airport:
The Hedon Aerodrome Saga

by

Alexander Slingsby

ISBN-13: 978-1-5262-0453-0

Please send e-mail enquiries to: *hedonaerodromesaga@gmail.com*

First published in Great Britain in 2016 by

Alexander Slingsby

In Memory of:

Albert Neville Medforth

(1924-2007)

I would like to thank the following for their support during the making of this book:

Dr Oliver Musgrave

East Riding Archive and Local Studies Service

Enviromail

Hymers College

Mr Eduard Winkler

Mr James Mitchell

Mr Paul Jackson

Mr Stuart Russell

Mr Tae Cragg

Mrs Ann Pattison

The Airfield Information Exchange

The Duke of Wellington's Regiment (West Riding)

The Hull Aero Club

The Hull Daily Mail

The Hull History Centre

The Ministry of Defence

The Prince of Wales's Own Regiment of Yorkshire Museum

Gustav Hamel photograph reproduced courtesy of Catherine Evans.

DEATH OF AN AIRPORT:

The Hedon Aerodrome Saga

Foreword

For all those readers familiar with Hedon and Paull Aerodrome, you might not be so familiar with their histories. That is because for the longest time, their stories remained vastly untold. As the grandson of Albert Neville Medforth, he played a prominent part in my life for many years. In July 2007 after a short stay in hospital, Neville passed away, leaving behind a great history that would not be known about until many years later.

Fast-forward to October 2014 when I decided to rummage, out of pure curiosity, through some of his belongings that had been kept. They had remained untouched since his death and I was curious to see what there was. What I uncovered turned out to be a vast, detailed history of events that only a few know the full extent of. Neville's keen enthusiasm for local aviation in the city of Kingston-upon-Hull led him to become involved with the Hedon Aerodrome in the late fifties, eventually paving the way for the creation of Paull Aerodrome in the late sixties. Not only did he keep all the documentation from his company, the *East Yorkshire Aero Company,* during its fifty years in operation, he had also kept meticulous diaries throughout these events.

Amongst the various papers and newspaper clippings, I found what appeared to be a book. It was unfinished, but from then on it was my aim to complete it in his memory, supplementing it with photographs and newer pieces of information. I hope that this book not only provides a detailed historical portrait of aviation within the city, but also a fitting tribute to my grandfather's devotion to aviation.

Alexander Slingsby

Contents

Chapter	Page
Who was Neville Medforth?	1
The Duke of Wellington's Regiment – A Brief Overview	8
Who was Neville Medforth? (Part II)	16
1957 – Initial Hedon Enquiries	27
1958 – Flying Begins from Hedon	30
1959 – An Objection from The Distillers Company	36
1960 – Appealing the Decision	51
1961 – Moving Forward	76
1962 – Flying Demonstration, RAF Pocklington and an Air Services Survey	90
1963 – Yeadon, RAF Pocklington and the Future of Hedon	102
1964 – One Last Flight from Hedon Aerodrome	110
1965 – Alternative Airfields including Wyton, Pocklington and Leconfield	120
1966 – The Future of Aviation in Hull, Paull and Autair International Airways	133
1967 – Paull, the Alternative to Hedon	141
1968 – Restarting at Paull	153
1969 – Flying Again	160
1970 – A Crisis	168
The Seventies – The Future of Paull and Humberside Airport	177
The Eighties – The End of Paull and an Alexandra Dock Helipad	182
The Nineties – One Last Attempt at Hedon	191

In Neville's own words…

Prologue	199
1. The Beginning	201
2. The True Facts	214
3. Trouble Beckons	223
4. Taking Stock	232
5. Hedon today, Paull tomorrow	236
6. The Beginning of the End	240
7. On Reflection	242

DEATH OF AN AIRPORT:

The Hedon Aerodrome Saga

Who was Neville Medforth?

Throughout the fifties, sixties and seventies, East Yorkshire resident Albert Neville Medforth campaigned tirelessly for a local air service to serve the people of Hull and its surrounding areas. He fought through trial and tribulation to see his dream come to fruition, but sadly was often financially prohibited from doing so.

Early Life

Neville was born at around 7.40 am on the morning of the 3 December 1924, to Emily (née Mowforth) and Albert Medforth, in a cottage down Ings Lane in the small village of Patrington, East Yorkshire. They had married two years earlier at the Patrington Village Church. A year later they had a daughter called June, and the family lived in Patrington until 1931. After moving to the village of Withernwick, Emily took up the position as Headmistress of the village school, retiring after thirty-two years of service in 1963.

Emily was a keen musician and, prior to the outbreak of war in 1939, performed as an amateur operatic soprano within societies across the East Riding and Hull. She was also a deputy church organist for several years, and acted as a choir conductor at the East Yorkshire branch of the Women's Institute. On the 17 September 1932, Emily gained an 'AMusLCM' Diploma from the London College of Music, a recognised qualification allowing her to support a musical career which enhanced her standing in the musical community.

His father Albert had fought in the First World War with the Nott's and Derby Regiment (The Sherwood Foresters) and later on in the 1940s became the Captain of the Withernwick Home Guard Platoon. He was a keen businessman and managed a Humber-based shipping firm, James Barraclough and Son. Founder of the company James Barraclough had also been one of the forefathers of the Hull City Football Club and throughout the twenties, managed a number of other corporations including an insurance firm. On the 29 May 1937, Albert christened a merchant vessel called the *Juneville*, named after his children. The launch took place in Beverley amidst great fanfare, with local press photographers present. Neville would later work for the company in the 1950s.

Launch of the *Juneville* – 29 May 1937

From the 17 September 1935 to 1941, Neville attended the independent school Hymers College in Kingston-upon-Hull, where he was admired by his peers for his artwork and his performances in athletics. His art usually consisted of suitably attired soldiers or explorers, and his exceptional performances in sport saw him crowned as champion of the Junior School in 1937. Indeed, records show that he was considered academically at the top of his class for Art in the same year. Whilst he undoubtedly took his schooling seriously, there was one incident during an assembly when another student made a remark which he had found somewhat amusing. Their behaviour had not gone unnoticed by the headmaster however and this resulted in both him and his peer receiving three strokes of the cane as punishment.

Although some students were evacuated with the outbreak of war in 1939, Neville's mother Emily made the decision to keep him at home and as such he continued to attend the school as normal until 1941. He often recalled his schooling experience as rather strict, but would continue his involvement with the institution as an 'Old Hymerian'. Regularly he would attend their sporting events and competed as part of their rugby team well into the seventies.

<u>Military Career</u>

After leaving school, Neville became involved with the armed forces. He had taken early training in the school's Cadet Corps in 1937 and then joined the Withernwick Home Guard in 1940. This lasted until he entered the army properly in 1943. In 1942, he became a member of the 298 (Hornsea) Squadron Air Training Corps (Hornsea Air Cadets), spending most of that year flying having passed full aircrew proficiency exams. He was enlisted into the army officially on the 15 May 1943.

Neville in RAF Uniform

Neville standing on a beach in
Palestine - September 1946

Neville considered surviving the Second World War as a frontline soldier a 'bonus'. From May 1944, he served as a footslogger in the 1st Battalion of the Duke of Wellington's Regiment, where he said things 'got tough on occasion'. Initially, he served as a rifleman in Italy, operating in Rome throughout June and July and later in Florence. After landing at Napoli in May and joining the Regiment at the Anzio beachhead, it is unclear as to whether he took part in the Battle of Anzio, although it is very likely that he did.

In October 1944, he suffered a minor leg injury which subsequently became infected. This could well have proved fatal, with antibiotics yet to be developed and with the only drugs available (such as prontosil) likely to have very little effect against bacteria. After being taken by air to a hospital back in Napoli, he then spent a somewhat unpleasant period of time recuperating in a Convalescent Depot, a makeshift hospital designed for wounded soldiers. Conditions were apparently so poor that the whole organisation was discussed in Parliament.

In February 1945, he departed for the Middle East. During this time, he served in countries such as Palestine, Syria and The Lebanon, as well as Egypt and The Sudan. His Battalion were involved in maintaining the peace whilst at the same time preventing the Haganah from training. They also assisted with the evacuation of French forces whilst under the watch of unfriendly journalists and constant heat in the summer months. It is expected that he had some very anxious moments during his service, but many good ones as well.

As a private he was commended for his admirable service, and described in a report produced upon his release from the army in July 1947 as an honest, reliable and efficient soldier. He was also said to be well liked and respected by both junior comrades and seniors alike. Earlier on during his service there had been a couple of minor incidents, most notably in June 1945 when he was awarded a detention lasting twenty-one days by the commanding officer, after he had failed to answer his name during a parade. Additionally, he was awarded a further fourteen days after being described as improperly dressed by wearing shorts whilst on active service, and using disobedient language toward a superior officer. Nevertheless, these minor incidents did not appear to have any marked effect upon his overall reputation, and his reference written at the end of his service made no mention of them.

He received four medals for his dutiful service on the 5 November 1948. These included the 1939-45 Star, the Italy Star, the Defence Medal and the War Medal (1939/45). He would later receive the General Service Medal and Clasp for his services in Palestine on the 8 November 1956.

DEATH OF AN AIRPORT:

The Hedon Aerodrome Saga

The Duke of Wellington's Regiment – A Brief Overview

A detailed account, written by one of the officers who served with the Battalion, during its stay in the Middle East is given below. This has been kindly provided by the Regimental Association of The Duke of Wellington's Regiment.

THE 1st BATTALION – 1945 TO 1947

Palestine, Syria, the Lebanon, Egypt and the Sudan

On 9 January, 1945, the 1st Battalion was in its battle positions in the Monte Grande sector, high in the Apennines in Italy, when the 85th (US) Division commenced its takeover from 1st (Br) Division. Elements of 337th Regimental Combat Team took over from the Battalion. As usual in such takeovers by the US Army, there were not enough slit trenches in my or other platoon positions to accommodate all the US soldiers. My Number 1 Platoon of A Company consisted of but twenty soldiers, whereas the American platoon was almost forty strong. However, somewhat churlishly, this was a problem that we had to leave to the Americans to dig themselves out of and we were thankful to trek down the mountainside to the vehicles waiting to take us down to Perugia, some 100 miles north of Rome. This was the start of our long journey to the Promised Land of Palestine.

On 7 February we entrained for a tediously slow 48 hour rail transit (40 Hommes ou 8 Chevaux – cattle trucks) from Perugia to Taranto, on the heel of Italy, arriving on 9 February. Also at Taranto was our old 4th Battalion, then entitled 58 Anti-Tank Regiment RA (DWR). After some ten days in a tented camp, along with HQ 3rd Brigade, 2 Foresters and I, we embarked aboard *SS Banfbra* reaching the port of Haifa on the morning of 22 February. A further rail journey took us to camp at Majdal in the south of the country.

Over this time Major Magill-Cuerdon of the Essex Regiment had been in command, having taken over from Lieutenant Colonel F P St Maur Shell DSO when he was killed in October on Monte Ceco, but he left us in November to take command of the 4th Essex. He was not with us for long but was well liked and the Battalion was sorry to see him go. Lieutenant Colonel B (Barney) McCall, a Royal Fusilier, took over in November and saw us to Palestine. He was a charming man, perhaps too quiet but he certainly understood the Battalion and its Yorkshire soldiers. Of slim build, grey haired and a most patient CO it was sad when, very much against his wishes, he left us in March, 1945 for a staff job at GHQ in Cairo. (After the war he was a regular attendee at the Officers' 1943/45 Dinner Club.) Major P G L (Pat) Cousens, a pre-war Duke, came as Second-in-Command, also in November – fresh from commanding a battalion in the Sudan Defence Force. (I met him for the first time on a snow covered platoon position on Monte Cerere when he toured the Battalion's area with the CO). He was quickly posted and did not travel to Palestine. There was an interregnum when Colonel McCall left the Battalion and Major T F (Freddie) Huskisson MC took over until Lieutenant Colonel C W G (Coot) Orr OBE arrived on 16 April 1945.

At this time two outstanding soldiers, both of great character, were awarded the MBE – RSM G W E (Joe) Annesley and RQMS E (Ted) Cherry. RSM Annesley joined the 3rd Battalion in July 1919 and then the 2nd Battalion in August, serving in Ireland, Egypt, Palestine and Singapore after which he joined the 15th Battalion, seeing service in Malta and then went with the Battalion to France on the outbreak of war, being one of those evacuated from Dunkirk. He remained with the Battalion through North Africa, Pantellaria and Italy. He was an imposing figure but, perhaps unusually, was always most kind to young subalterns. More practically he ensured that the forward companies were never short of ammunition supplies. A useful rugby player, he was capped for the Army against the RAF in 1931. RQMS Cherry was a veteran of WW1 and transferred from The West Yorkshire Regiment in 1919, serving continuously with the Battalion for all of 26 years, celebrating his quarter century with the Battalion on the Anzio Beachhead, while in peacetime he had soldiered in Ireland, Gibraltar, Turkey and Malta. He too had been at Dunkirk, North Africa and Italy. Both were venerable gentlemen in their late forties and they made a good team under Major H J T Sills MC, who joined in 1940 from the HAC and who commanded HQ Company and looked after 'B' Echelon, a most onerous task, in Italy when it was compounded by the difficult job of organising the mule trains to ensure supplies were got forward to the line. Also, at this time, another long serving Duke left the Regiment for civilian life. This was ORQMS 'Sam' Ambler who was based at Offices 2nd Echelon (02E), GHQ Middle East Forces, and Cairo. Perforce he was seen only rarely but did sterling service looking after the Battalion's administrative and manpower needs throughout the war.

Once installed in our tented camp at Majdal we took over our Internal Security (IS) duties, being well briefed by the Palestine Police on our main role of covering the entry of illegal immigrants and the more dangerous role of combating the Stern Gang, a vicious organisation already notorious for the assassination of Lord Moyne, the British Resident Minister in Cairo in November 1944, as well as the Haganah. The Stern Gang was a breakaway faction of the Irgun (Irgun Zwai Leumi or National Military Organisation) whilst the Haganah, initially raised before the war by Orde Wingate, primarily for the defence of Jewish settlements against the Arabs, had become increasingly militant against the British Army. Many of its members were former members of the Palmach and the Jewish Brigade which had fought in Italy in the 8th Army with General Alexander. All three organisations had rejected the Jewish Agency's policy of restraint against the British and the Arabs, with the Irgun resorting to indiscriminate revenge bombings, the killing of Arabs, also raiding RAF airfields, stealing arms from military bases and killing British soldiers and kidnapping officers. April 1946 saw the Irgun kill seven soldiers of 6th Airborne Division in an army car park in Tel Aviv.

With this as a background the Battalion trained for IS duties, involving the now outdated platoons in squares, together with the reading of the Riot Act by a magistrate before the opening of fire was threatened. The Battalion never fired a single shot against the Jews but a soldier in 2nd Foresters mistakenly fired a shot in the air, wounding some person on a balcony in Haifa. One of the important security roles was to prevent the Haganah training in the hills and open country, resulting in my being given command of 'Z' Platoon, mounted in carriers and manned mainly by the Intelligence Section with the remit to find illegal training. We covered many miles all over southern Palestine but achieved nothing. However, the main activity of the Battalion arose whenever an illegal ship arrived off the coast of Palestine. Such ships were usually shadowed by the Royal Navy, but often illegal immigrants scrambled ashore and efforts were made to intercept them. Once or twice the battalion had to go aboard these ships to ensure none escaped before the ship was made to turn round and then proceed to Cyprus where the Jews were disembarked into a refugee camp. This was an unsavoury business, not relished by officers and men alike, as most of the refugees were in a pitiful state after their long and harrowing journey from Europe. A disturbing factor was that all our activities were watched by journalists from the unfriendly Washington Post and the New York Times who were responsible for distributing their anti-British articles and pictures around both the western and the Arab worlds.

But, before all this activity which was the Battalion's normal role in Palestine, the Battalion in June and July was deployed to Syria to help with the evacuation of both the French forces and French officers serving with native troops, because the French mandate had been ended. This entailed escorting and protecting convoys from Damascus, where the Battalion was encamped on the racecourse, to the docks at Beirut. Later the Battalion moved to the pine forests above Beirut, giving much opportunity to visit the town although the French influence was still strong and the British were distinctly unwelcome. Beirut was also most expensive and the £18 sterling per month allowed by the Field Cashier for a subaltern did not stretch very far in the up-market bars, hotels and restaurants.

After the venture into Syria the Battalion was back in Palestine, stationed first outside Tel Aviv in August and then, in October, at Haifa on Mount Carmel. On 12 December 1945, when the Division was relieved by 3rd Infantry Division, there was a welcome road and rail move to Moascar on the West Bank of the Suez Canal in Egypt, alongside the Greek-French Arab town of Ismailia. This was a peacetime, pre-war garrison camp with proper office buildings, barrack rooms and houses with much comfort appropriate to the 'good old days'.

By May 1946, the Battalion was back in Palestine in Peninsular Barracks, Haifa, again a peace time camp, on the edge of the sea and (tactically more importantly) within a few minutes of the centre of Haifa. The time in Haifa was often spent in intense IS duties and, because of the serious situation, caused a ruling that soldiers should only go into town in pairs and fully armed. Guards on Vital Points, patrols and road blocks were frequent occurrences. At times the town was put out of bounds and the arrival of a ship carrying illegal immigrants invariably meant the Battalion turning out for a period of 24 hours or longer. Demobilisation was in full swing and this entailed the reduction of the Battalion from six companies down to four, with Support Company's mortars, carriers and pioneers being devolved to the rifle companies. Much promotion ensued (including Isles to be Captain & Adjutant) owing to leave to UK and demobilisation. On 29 June there was a huge security operation throughout Palestine with the ambitious aim of capturing, in their beds, some very important Jews (Vt.s). Despite close security surrounding the operation the terrorist Jews were alerted and even after a thorough combing of the town of Haifa the Battalion had no success, although in many houses, warm beds and half-eaten meals on tables were found. It was a great disappointment.

In October Lieutenant Colonel C R T (Dick) Cumberlege took over command from Lieutenant Colonel Orr, and Major T St G Carroll became Second-in Command. WOI Banks arrived from UK and became RSM., taking over from RSM O'Shea. The Battalion had been destined for the Canal Zone in the middle of November but, on 1 November, when the Battalion was deployed on operational duties in Haifa, with Battalion HQ located at the railway station and the rifle companies engaged in searches and patrols in the town, the CO was called to Brigade HQ and told to prepare the Battalion for an air move to Khartoum in the Sudan on 7 November. This necessitated frantic activity by the Orderly Room and resulted in an impeccable Operation Order involving innumerable Appendices which was largely due to the CO's wealth of knowledge on such intricate movement matters. The Advance Party left in one plane on 6 November and the Battalion in Halifaxes and Lancasters on the 7th. The thousand-mile trip was covered in six hours in good flying conditions. The Rear Party, after an arduous rail and River Nile journey arrived on 24 November.

The reason for our move to Khartoum was never fully explained, although rumours were heard that civil unrest was feared. This never materialised and certainly all was quiet and peaceful both on our arrival and throughout our stay in the station. North Barracks on the north bank of the Blue Nile was, unfortunately, large enough to accommodate only HQ and 'A' Companies, and 'C' and 'D' Companies had to live with the RAF on the opposite bank of the river. In February 1947, Lieutenant Colonel B W Webb-Carter DSO OBE, our old wartime leader, took over from Colonel Dick Cumberlege who left for a staff appointment in Suez. The Colonel also brought with him a selection of Mess silver, preceded by Major C F Grieve with the Colours. With the reformation of the Drums

Platoon it was apparent that the Battalion was returning to a welcome peacetime routine. The Drums beat Reveille every Saturday morning and also led the Battalion on a 'Flag March' through the town, an event which produced many spectators from the populace. Because of an influx of airmen to the RAF, 1st 'D' Company, under Major Grieve, had to move into camp at Gebeit, located some 90 miles to the north-west of Port Sudan, in the Red Sea Hills, then to be followed by 'C' and 'A' Companies in rotation.

This was a pleasant, cooler station than Khartoum and enabled much training, including field firing to take place. Highlights of 1947 included a ceremonial parade for General Sir Miles Dempsey, GOC-in-C Middle East Land Forces, on 12 January. This was the first time the Colours had been paraded since before the war and was, thus, an historic occasion. Commanded by Lieutenant Colonel Cumberlege, with the Band of the Sudan Defence Force also on parade, it evinced high praise from the GOC-in-C. On 5 April HE the Governor, General and Lady Huddleston, left Khartoum by air at the end of a lifetime's service in The Sudan, where he had commanded the Camel Corps and held the appointment of Kaid and GOC. The Battalion furnished a Guard of Honour commanded by Major RE Austin. (His successor, a former Labour MP arrived by train at 0600 hours, dressed in a morning coat and, it is said, remarked to the Kaid, "You're used to hunting and shooting, while I am used to shunting and tooting." (Being an ex-engine driver!) Again the Battalion provided a Guard of Honour.

Khartoum proved to be a happy station for the Battalion and a great deal of sport was played, including polo for the CO and one or two other officers. The heat was intense in the summer months and ran at about 100+ degrees Fahrenheit with, all too often, the Haboob, the notorious sand storm of this part of Africa making life almost intolerable for two or three days on end. We were fortunate in having our old friends of 1st Battalion The King's Shropshire Light Infantry located in South Barracks and we saw much of them.

By 16 November, 1947, the Battalion was back in the UK and stationed at Proteus Camp, Ollerton, Notts.

DEI

Written 2 April 2008

DEATH OF AN AIRPORT:

The Hedon Aerodrome Saga

Who was Neville Medforth?

<u>After the War</u>

After being demobbed in 1947 and 'not knowing what to do', Neville applied to and was interviewed at various teacher training colleges. Failing to get in at St. John's College in York, a last minute vacancy came up at Saltley College in Birmingham due to a cancellation. For two years he trained to become a schoolmaster, qualifying in 1949. In December 1949, he married and would later have two children. Owing to a low salary and with a young family, he left teaching and switched to commerce in the early 1950s. In 1960, he was to remarry and have a further three children.

In the fifties, Neville continued his military involvement within the Territorial Army, serving with the 4th Battalion East Yorkshire Regiment. According to the March 1952 edition of *The Snapper* (the East Yorkshire regimental magazine), in 1951 he was called up as a 'Z' Reservist and volunteered for the Territorial

Army. He served in 'B' Company and had recently been commissioned into the Battalion as a 2nd Lieutenant.

[Courtesy of the Hull Daily Mail]

Presentation of the Colours to the 4th Battalion – The Lord Lieutenant presenting the Queen's Colour to the Ensign, Lieut. A.N. Medforth

He is first shown in the army list as being appointed a lieutenant with effect from the 15 December 1951. The Battalion attended its annual camp based in Wiltshire in 1953, which lasted from 5 to 18 July. An account appeared in the August edition of *The Snapper* and a named photograph of the Battalion's officers was included, in which Neville is included. Perhaps his proudest moment with the Battalion came on the 19 September 1953, when the Regiment were presented with the Queen's Colour at West Park in Hull. An account published in *The Snapper* shows Neville as one of the two junior officers privileged in carrying the Colour.

The ceremony was attended by the Lord Lieutenant of the East Riding of Yorkshire, Colonel Michael Willoughby, 11th Baron Middleton who himself held an impressive military career, commanding the 5th and 30th Battalions of the East Yorkshire Regiment during the Second World War. Later on in 1957, Colonel Willoughby was awarded the honourable title of Knight of the Garter, the oldest and most senior British order of chivalry honouring those who have either held public office and contributed to national life, or who have served the Sovereign personally. Neville is seen in a photograph receiving the Colour from Colonel Willoughby, as well as appearing in two further photographs carrying the Colour on parade.

Middle: Colours presented to the Battalion by Colonel the Lord Middleton, M.C., T.D. 19 September 1953. Colour Party: Lieuts. Medforth and Bridger, C.M.S.s Smith, Bowden and Wright. – **Top**: The Lord Lieutenant addresses the Battalion after presenting the New Colours. [Courtesy of the Yorkshire Post]

The December 1953 edition of *The Snapper* recorded the Battalion's annual prize giving. Neville is recorded as having won the Earle Trophy and also a silver spoon as the Battalion's best officer in rifle shooting. He was promoted to Captain from the 1 February 1954 and appointed second in command of 'B' Company. He was also involved in the Battalion seven-a-side rugby team that was to take part in a competition at Bridlington.

The 4th Battalion East Yorkshire Regiment – Summer Camp 1954

The Battalion's annual camp in 1954 was held at Fylingdales. A named photograph of the officers was included in *The Snapper* and Neville is included. In September 1954, the results of the Queen's Challenge Cup were announced, with the Battalion coming sixth amongst the national Territorial Army units, in which he was noted. On 18 December 1955, the Battalion held its annual prize presentation and he received trophies from the T.A.S.A. (Territorial Army Sports Association).

During the T.A.S.A. meeting of 1956, Neville won the competition's javelin and discus events, as well as coming third in the shot-put. The annual camp that year was again at Fylingdales and began on the 30 June. He is recorded in the regimental journal as being a chief weapons instructor, but the type of weapon is not recorded. On the 23 September, the Battalion took part in the annual shooting contest with the Kingston-upon-Hull police force, where he achieved the highest score. He would also be crowned the winner of that year's Major Shaw Cup. In June 1957, Neville captained the Battalion's athletics team in which he was again most successful, as recorded by *The Snapper*. The annual camp that year was held in Whitburn, with training exercises taking place with the Royal Artillery at Otterburn and at R.A.F. Middleton St George.

The Regiment won the Queen's Challenge Cup for that year, with the trophy being competed for by all of the territorial units in Great Britain and Northern Ireland. Neville was highly successful in the T.A.'s athletics championship and the points he gained contributed to the winning of the cup. In January 1959 the Battalion's annual prize presentation took place, where he received a trophy as Captain of the athletics team. In September 1959, he won a pistol firing competition at Whitburn.

In September 1960, Neville joined the Royal Engineers as Lieutenant Medforth. His seniority in the Royal Engineers was the same as when he joined the 4th Battalion East Yorkshire Regiment, almost a decade earlier. In the March 1961 army list, he is shown as serving with the Royal Engineers but in the September 1962 army list he no longer appears, so presumably he had retired from the Territorial Army at some point. It is possible that this change from infantry to engineers came about when Neville moved from Hornsea to Hull, and it was more convenient for him to join a local engineer unit. As he had no engineer experience he would probably have had to join at a lower rank.

Caricatures of the 4th Battalion East Yorkshire Regiment at Fylingdales Camp –
June 1956

Sporting Career

As a keen sportsman going back to his schooldays, Neville began competing in athletics and rugby 'as a way of keeping fit'. In July 1953, he took part in the Territorial Army's athletic championships, gaining a record result in the discus and also winning the shot-put event. His achievements would later be featured in *The Services and Territorial Magazine* (Vol. 22, No. 210) where he was commended as the 'burly Neville Medforth'.

In 1956, he competed in the Yorkshire County Athletic Championships, which were held at the Leeds' Municipal Athletic Ground on the 2 June. Representing the Hull Spartan Athletic Club, Neville competed in various events including the 120 Yard Hurdle (Event 13), Pole Vault (17), Hammer Throw (18), Discus (20), Shot-put (22) and Javelin (24), coming seventh, third, third, seventh, ninth and fifth respectively.

His passion in athletics was recognised in 1951 when he was invited by Mr D.E. Noel-Paton, then Director of the Lectures Department at The British Council, to discuss a proposal which would see a British representative visiting Nigeria for two months. Said representative would give sports coaching and try and raise the standard of athletic training within the country. This had been arranged by then Principal Mr Bouffler of the Carnegie College of Physical Education (now Leeds Beckett University). The eight-week period was planned so said individual could travel around the northern, western and eastern provinces to allow coaching across the country. It is unknown, however, whether he took up this opportunity.

His sporting activities also took him overseas and on the 26 July 1957, playing as part of the Hull Spartan Athletics Club, he competed against the Aachen and District Team in Aachen, Germany. The German team won the tournament with

141 points, 13 points ahead of the Hull team, but it was reportedly a close contest for a while. Neville achieved the top distance for the English competitors in the shot-put (12.45 metres) but was beaten by Buntzel of Aachen with his first and best shot – 12.75m (Buntzel was not able to get any closer to his personal best of that year, which was 13.54m).

In the discus and javelin events, the English team also reigned supreme and Neville won the discus with an outstanding long distance throw of 40.89m – the best performance from the Aachen club being Rothstein with a mere 34.39m. Third in this event was another member of the Hull team, Thomson, with 32.96m. The top performance in the javelin by Neville's teammate Thomson with 45.32m was rather average in comparison. The English team also won the final event, the 4 x 100m relay with a speed of 44.2 seconds against 44.4 seconds for the Aachen team. The following Sunday, the Hull team participated in another athletics tournament in Eschweiler (a nearby town).

Neville 'throwing the hammer' at an event in Eschweiler, 28 July 1957

Throughout the sixties, Neville was actively involved with the Hull Spartan Athletic Club, contributing to their events and coaching, including a number of visiting German athletes in the latter part of the decade. His participation in athletics continued into the seventies, when on the 11 June 1971, he was featured in the athletics section of the Hull Daily Mail. The article highlighted how out of the eight events to be staged, the men's discus event had provoked the most interest. Hull Spartan the 'evergreen Nev Medforth' was expected to secure maximum points. On the 19 May 1973, he would compete in the Track and Field Championships, held by the Yorkshire County Amateur Athletic Association at the Clairville Stadium in Middlesbrough. Now classed as a senior participant, he competed in the shot-put, hammer throw and discus events, coming seventh, ninth and seventh respectively. Neville, now in his fifties, began to wind down his participation in sports somewhat, but still keenly followed the news of various sports worldwide.

In February 1972, he began to make preparations for a solo crossing of the North Sea, which would see him launch from Hull at the end of April and arrive in Oslo, Norway by the 17 May. He had intended to row the entire distance in a small rowing boat, and if he felt 'fresh enough' would endeavour to return in the same way. The boat builders were to be Pebble Boats of Westgate, who were based in the seaside town of Hornsea. The company, jointly owned by two well-known Hornsea men Joe Gelsthorpe and Geoff Southwell, had been formed in 1970 to produce and manufacture the pebble design fishing craft.

Neville's idea behind the crossing was not purely for fitness purposes; but he felt that useful scientific data such as sea samples for pollution tests could be collected for examination. He also felt that the trip could potentially encourage trade relations between the cities. Trying to drum up support and potential sponsorship, he wrote to the Director of Programming at Yorkshire Television, Mr Donald Baverstock, and the Press Association, hoping that any publicity would result in sponsorship for his endeavours. Mr Baverstock responded favourably, stating that there was potential news interest and a news report was produced as part of their daily news programme *Calendar* later that year. Rather unfortunately, the crossing did not take place and the most likely reason for this was that the sponsorship required in making the crossing did not come through as hoped.

On the 22 April 1972, an article about the planned crossing was featured in the local newspaper, in which he told a reporter 'I admit to being forty' when in reality he was forty-eight. The article stated how he hoped to tackle the 'lonely row' in a sixteen-foot wooden boat and was looking for sponsors to cover the costs of the trip, estimated at over £1,000. The article had revealed how Neville had been training hard at Hornsea, in which he stated, 'I have been out in some fairly rough seas and have gone out as far as ten miles.' He added, 'I have rowed for twenty-five years – I used to be in the Army cutter crews and I am certain I can do this… I have studied several books on tides and currents and I am sure that I can use them to my best advantage.'

The boat in question would be fully equipped with rescue apparatus and food supplies designed to last three weeks in either direction. Whilst the North Sea was busy with shipping, the possibility of being hit did not frighten him. 'It's a very big place indeed. For a ship to hit a boat the size of mine would be a remote chance indeed.'

DEATH OF AN AIRPORT:

The Hedon Aerodrome Saga

1957

A small site outside the East Yorkshire village of Hedon was used as the Kingston-upon-Hull municipal airport up until the outbreak of the Second World War in 1939. The flag carrier airline KLM operated there between 1934 and 1935 using Fokker three-engine high-wing monoplanes, but discontinued the service due to lack of passengers. During the war, the airfield was converted into a training ground and used by the War Department, who installed various gun pits and huts. After the war the Hull Corporation, who then owned the airfield, could not restart flying due to lack of funding and from then on, the land was used for farming.

Neville could recall his earliest memory of aviation, witnessing an air display at the age of five years old at the Hedon Aerodrome in 1930. Twenty-seven years later, he was back at the site assessing its suitability for flying. On the 17 January 1957, he wrote to then Town Planning Officer at the Hull Corporation, Mr Harold F. Alston, expressing initial interest in the site and querying if the field would be available for lease or for use by light aircraft.

The Hull Corporation around this time had been investigating the possibility of a helicopter service for the city. In May 1955, a council committee meeting had concluded that Sammy's Point would be the most suitable site for the provision of helicopter facilities, although it had been argued by the then Chief Executive of British European Airways, that the development of aircraft used to ensure a commercial success of the service had proved 'disappointingly slow'. He had similarly suggested that it would not be for another decade until helicopters were a possibility on the domestic network, although he had not abandoned hope that cities such as Hull would one day be linked by this means of travel. Nevertheless in his letter to Mr Alston, Neville argued that whilst back then he was interested in a proposed helicopter base, the drawback in his view was the purchase and running costs of the helicopters themselves. He also felt helicopters were a novelty and ill-equipped in the event of engine failure.

Hull at the time did not have a dedicated airport and Neville had hoped that the Hedon site could be rejuvenated for the operation of light aircraft. The most expensive item of purchase, he stressed, would be the commercial pilot, and arguing that potential sources of income could be obtained through club flying, membership fees, local air services, charter work and agricultural crop spraying. He estimated that the initial set-up costs would be around £3-5,000.

A week or so after writing to the Hull Corporation, Neville visited the aerodrome site and inspected its suitability for flying himself. After a fairly comprehensive survey, he concluded that the field was in a good enough condition to operate a light airfield, and added that only a small portion of the site (around a hundred acres) would be required to do so. He remarked that the aging pre-war hangar was in a reasonable condition, but would need some work to allow a plane to taxi from it onto the field. At the back of the hangar were several sizeable rooms, along with two huts, which he stated could be used as part of a flying club. A platform for the Hull to Withernsea railway line was handily opposite the site and this, he argued, could be a useful commodity once an airfield was established. The flying approach from all sides was excellent in his view, with no telegraph poles or other obstacles affecting this.

With the site at Hedon only four miles from Hull City Centre, Neville argued that few other cities had the luxury of aeroplane travel within such close proximity. Indeed, the only other alternative would be a helicopter station, which he discredited. At around the same time, he purchased a small aeroplane as an indication of his own enthusiasm for the project and was exploring the possibility of operating it from Hedon. The plane, a de Havilland Tiger Moth DE638, had been purchased for the sum of £50, and had previously been used by the Royal Air Force and the Fleet Air Arm (FAA) during the Second World War, as a means of providing basic flying training for recruits.

In the middle of 1957, senior officials at the Hull Corporation including the Town Clerk and the Town Planning Officer were in agreement that firmer proposals would need to be submitted by him, in order for the Corporation to consider whether they would make the Hedon site available. In any event, the officials stressed that they could not provide any financial support for the endeavour, and for the proposal to even be considered, Neville would need to handle all financial aspects of the plan himself. The Town Planning Department dealt with the application until the middle of 1958, when it was passed on to the City Treasurer.

DEATH OF AN AIRPORT:

The Hedon Aerodrome Saga

1958

1958 would be an even busier year for Neville as he began to make significant progress with his plans for Hedon Aerodrome. In June of that year, he made contact with a dairy farmer by the name of Mr Stamford Smith, regarding the grazing rights on the site. Mr Smith was opposed to any flying at Hedon, as his cattle of around 200-300 would have be unable to graze the land. In July, Neville again wrote to the Town Planning Officer at the Hull Corporation, stating that he intended to form a flying club based at the former airfield, which he hoped would build up interest locally. Later on, the airfield was inspected by an official from the Ministry of Aviation and, despite the Ministry suggesting that slight surface work be carried out as well as improvements to the rescue equipment and boundary markers, they considered the airfield suitable for flying.

It was hoped that the club would operate at weekends and already owning one aircraft allowed them to make a start. In a letter, Neville appealed to the council for an amount of 'goodwill and understanding' as he felt it would be too expensive to pay rent and rates for just weekend use. Following on from his contact with Mr Smith in June, the farmer was apparently unwilling to become involved with the flying scheme and this difference of opinion caused a divide between the two parties that would become much more dramatic in the months ahead.

In a letter dated the 16 July, Neville wrote to the Ministry of Transport and Civil Aviation asking for advice on his proposals. A few days later, divisional controller Mr Hullock recommended to him that a licensed aerodrome catering for flying instruction should contain at least two strips of land, 300 feet wide at right angles to each other with one being 600 yards long and the other being slightly less. These figures were based on the aircraft the club had planned on using at the time, a Tiger Moth.

He suggested that should any fencing be required along the edges of each strip, to contain grazing stock, these fences must not subtend a greater angle than 1 in 7 from the strip edge. If there were to be fences at both sides, they must have a distance between them of at least 350 feet. Mr Hullock confirmed his intention to inspect the Hedon Aerodrome on the 7 August and following this, Neville officially submitted his flying club proposals. These were sent to the Town Planning Officer at the Hull Corporation.

His proposals, outlined in one page, included the arrangements of rent on the airfield, proposals for the former hangar, a club house, the club's title, proposed members of the club and the club's constitution. The rent, subject to an agreement with the Hull Corporation, Mr Smith and the flying club, outlined how the club was prepared to pay whatever amount was decided, based on Mr Smith's grazing inconveniences at weekends. The Territorial and Auxiliary Forces Association had also agreed to allow the club to use the hangar for aircraft storage, subject to the Hull Corporation's approval.

It was decided that a hut near the hangar would be suitable for use as a clubhouse, but would require some attention prior to being used. The club name was to be the East Yorkshire Aero Club and an application was put forward to the Association of British Aero Clubs under this title. Supporters were also listed in this letter, which included a number of flyers and non-flyers. Following on from the proposals being submitted, Neville received swift confirmation of the Town Planning Committee's favourable stance towards them, although this stance was subject to suitable financial arrangements being put in place. The City Treasurer at the time was instructed to investigate the financial arrangements between the club, the Corporation and the existing tenant of the land.

During late 1958, a number of verbal discussions took place between Neville and the City Treasurers Department. Initially concerning the area which was to be used for flying, it was stipulated by the Corporation that this area be kept as small as possible, and quite a bit of work was involved to implement this request. Mr Allon, a Manager at the Distillers Company Limited (DCL) had enquired as to whether the plan could be modified in the corner, adjacent to the company's sports ground, to ensure aircraft avoided coming too close to it. In the end, the Ministry of Aviation came to the rescue and a much simpler plan was submitted.

On the 1 December 1958, an official go-ahead was given by the Hull Corporation, allowing the East Yorkshire Aero Club to use the former airfield as a flying club and training school. This was the decision Neville had been waiting for, and it was confirmed in a letter sent by the City Treasurer, Mr C.H. Pollard, C.B.E. The letter explicitly stated that the Corporation was willing to allow the use of the land at £350 per year in rent and that they would make a rare exception in allowing the flying club to sub-let the land back to the then tenant farmer, Mr Smith. This was providing it was grazed when not being used by the club itself.

The original airfield plan had been amended after the Hull Corporation had refused the club to sub-let a larger area of land. Likening the amended plans to

33

an unfinished jigsaw puzzle, they had been composed of various one hundred yard wide strips which were deliberately planned in the smallest area to allow student pilots to be taught. Mr Smith agreed to become a sub-tenant of the flying club and consequently his cattle grazed the flying club part of the land within agreed times. A fence was installed running north to south, to the east of the flying club's area.

All of these events were described in a letter by Neville to Mr C.L. Hullock, four months after their original meeting. He revealed that he had approached Morton Air Services, one of the earliest post-World War Two independent British airlines, about not only supporting the flying club, but to find out whether it would be worthwhile opening the airfield for light commercial air traffic. He similarly approached several other companies enquiring about this.

Originally, the club wished to lease a rectangular area between two fences amounting to little over a hundred acres. The Corporation would not allow this and instead pressured the club to reduce this to the smallest possible size. A further piece was taken out of the sports field area, ensuring that no planes would be able to fly near or taxi there, at the request of the neighbouring Distillers Company. As this would result in the north to south run being less than five hundred yards, Mr Allon agreed to allow a wedge further east, so that a five hundred yard run could be performed there instead.

Top: Hull Road, Hedon – picture taken over Hedon, looking west, the aerodrome is on the right side of the picture. [Courtesy of the Hull Daily Mail, 1970]

Bottom: The former Hedon airfield, taken from the former Hull to Withernsea Railway track bed. [Courtesy of Andy Beecroft]

Telephone No. 36880
(Guildhall, Hull)

C. H. POLLARD, C.B.E.
F.I.M.T.A. F.S.A.A.
CITY TREASURER

REGISTRAR OF STOCK.
CHIEF RATING OFFICER.
VALUATION OFFICER.
LOCAL TAXATION OFFICER.

Our Ref. WJA/ES/8/ES.145

Your Ref.

ALL COMMUNICATIONS TO BE ADDRESSED TO THE CITY TREASURER.

P.O. BOX No. 15,
GUILDHALL
KINGSTON UPON HULL

1st December, 1958.

Dear Sir,

Aerodrome Site, Hedon
Suggested Flying Club

    I have to refer to correspondence which has passed between yourself and departments of the Corporation and to discussions which you have had with my assistant in the above matter. On the basis of the plan, copy enclosed herewith, which you left with me showing the minimum area edged internally in pink which you would require for flying facilities, totalling approximately 57 acres, I would be prepared to recommend to the appropriate Committee of the Corporation that you should be afforded the use of the land subject to payment of a rental of £350 per annum, and to you being responsible also for the payment of any rates which may become due. It is not the custom of the Corporation to permit sub-letting of any land or property in their ownership, but I feel that in the circumstances connected with your proposed occupation they would be prepared to make an exception on this occasion, provided that the land was grazed when not in actual use by you which is essential if the land is to be kept in good order and prevent the growth of weeds which would have an adverse effect on the value of the land for future grazing. The rental would be payable quarterly in advance on the 1st January, 1st April, 1st July and 1st October, and I feel that the Committee would call also for guarantors.

    I must point out that no access to the land to be used by you will be available from Hull Road, Hedon, and all members of the proposed Flying Club must be made aware of this, as the Corporation could not permit any interference with the grazing rights over the remainder of the aerodrome site which will be exercised by a farmer.

    I understand it to be the intention of the proposed Club to house aircraft in the Hangar at present on land leased from the Corporation by the Territorial and Auxiliary Forces Association for the East Riding, but before this could be accomplished or any use be made of the land and buildings at present on lease to the Association, it will be necessary for the Corporation to authorise such use.

    I shall be glad to hear from you so soon as you have had an opportunity of considering the matter so that I can obtain the instructions of the appropriate Committee thereon.

                    Yours faithfully,

                    C. H. Pollard

             City Treasurer.

The original 'go-ahead' letter, sent by Mr C.H. Pollard, C.B.E., the City Treasurer of the Hull Corporation – 1 December 1958.

DEATH OF AN AIRPORT:

The Hedon Aerodrome Saga

1959

1959 had initially begun with great optimism, with Neville swiftly accepting the Hull Corporation offer to use fifty-seven acres of the Hedon Aerodrome site. Within the first few months, the club received a large amount of interest from both flyers and non-flyers and at one point had seventy-eight members. The year would also see the first appearance of the flying club in the press, when on the 15 May 1959 an article was featured in a local newspaper entitled 'Tiger Moth dropped in on Hedon', accompanied by a photograph of the flying club's directors.

At around 8.30 pm the night before, Neville had landed at Hedon in his Tiger Moth aeroplane, surprising the village's residents. A local was so shocked that they contacted the police and a sergeant and constable were dispatched to investigate. It is possible that due to low cloud, the crew were forced to fly low resulting in the plane being more noticeable than usual. The Tiger Moth was to be one of several planes the club had planned on purchasing, and on that night they had visited Ingoldmells, Skegness to pick up the silver, two-seater aircraft. Accompanying for the flight was newly appointed director Mr William K. Charles (more commonly known as Ken Charles), a Royal Air Force serviceman and passenger of the East Yorkshire Aero Club's first ever voyage. The then chief test pilot of Blackburn Aircraft, Mr Tim Wood, was said to also become the main flying instructor at the flying club. The aircraft company were willing to provide a subsidised scheme at the airfield that would see the training of potential employees to fly.

Tiger Moth dropped in on Hedon

15ᵗʰ MAY 1959

A PLANE LANDED AT HEDON AIRFIELD last night—and that surprised the inhabitants. For the airfield now is strictly for the cows. They were so surprised that one man telephoned Hedon police, who sent a sergeant and a constable to see what it was all about.

The explanation was quite simple.

The plane—a little Tiger Moth—belongs to the newly-formed East Yorkshire Aero Club, Ltd.

MANAGING DIRECTOR

They had leased a portion of the old landing ground from Hull Corporation, and the plane was the first of several they plan to buy for their members.

The managing director, 32-year-old Mr Neville Medforth, who works for a Hull rivercraft firm, went down to Skegness to take delivery of the silver two-seater aircraft, and with RAF National Serviceman, Ken Charles, of 63, Cranswick-gr., Hull, as passenger, flew it up to Hedon. Charles, who is on leave, is a qualified pilot.

They touched down at 8.30 as the light was failing.

"We had to keep low all the way because of low cloud," Mr Medforth explained.

SAFELY LOCKED UP

Now G-ANEJ is safely chocked up and locked up in the airfield's small hanger—and Hedon should soon be accustomed to seeing planes circling their airfield once more.

LEAVING THE PLANE.—Mr N. Medforth (right) and AC K. Charles (left) leaving their Tiger Moth after last night's flight from Skegness to Hedon.

Hull Daily Mail article 'Tiger Moth dropped in on Hedon', 15 May 1959.

[Courtesy of the Hull Daily Mail]

Top: Hedon Aerodrome, 8 pm Friday 15 May 1959 – Left: Ken Charles, Harry Vidler, Ken Beverley and Neville Medforth. **Bottom**: Neville's Tiger Moth.

By late April, work began on renovating the airfield for operation, with the club intending to open by the 1 May. Electric and water were installed in the hangar, and a hut was also converted into a clubhouse. Over a hundred tonnes of concrete and rubbish were removed from the site and a number of craters were filled in.

Everything appeared to be going well, until without warning telegraph poles with overhead wires were installed by the British Transport Commission on the side of the Hull to Withernsea railway line. These were designed to replace old underground cables, which had been in use since the thirties. Upon noticing the work, the club quickly contacted Mr I.G. McGregor, a traffic manager at British Railways, to inform him of the hazard that these would cause. The Hull Corporation were apparently unaware poles were being installed, and an informal arrangement with the railway company some years prior ensured wires would be installed underground to protect the airfield's approaches. Clearly, this was an issue that needed to be resolved.

The club argued that the installation of these poles would not only pose a serious hazard to the whole of the airfield's northern approach, but all flying could have potentially been stopped as they were not present when the airfield was originally inspected. It was later argued that the installation of the poles contravened a pre-war agreement regarding airfield approaches and this ultimately meant a strip of land 100 yards by 600 yards situated next to the railway line was now unusable for flying. By January 1960, the British Transport Commission had agreed to remove the poles.

A working committee was formed to speed up progress on work to be completed prior to the club being opened to the public. Overall responsibility rested with Neville, but under him there were a number of committee members in charge of designated roles. The proposed working committee was as follows:

MR NEVILLE MEDFORTH	:	Executive Manager.
MR TED FARGUS	:	Boundary Markers and Signal Square.
KEN CHARLES	:	Map Room and Crew Room.
EDDIE ELSOM	:	Taxiways and Gap.

The above four members also formed a sub-committee responsible for the clearance of the airfield and its preparation for Ministry of Transport and Civil Aviation approval.

PAUL ELSOM	:	Windows and Doors (all buildings).
DON ASKEM)	:	Lighting (all buildings).
FRED STRICKLAND)		Repairs to Hangar Floor.
KEN BEVERLEY)	:	Strengthening of clubhouse floor
COLIN WRAY)		in preparation for covering.
DENNIS REED	:	Notice Boards and Signs.
BRIAN HEMMERMAN	:	Interior Decoration.

In June, Neville was advised that planning permission would now be required to resume use of the land as an airfield. A routine inspection from a representative of the Holderness Rural District Council led to the issue being brought up. The official, who was inspecting the petrol store, casually asked him whether planning permission had been applied for. Neville stated that he did not consider this to be a necessity, as the Hull Corporation had given the club written permission to start some months prior.

After further consideration, it was felt by all parties that there would be no harm in applying for this and that it would potentially be beneficial for the club in the long term. The Hull Corporation did not feel permission was required as it was an old municipal airport, but the East Riding County Council disagreed. Wanting to start as soon as possible, an application was submitted under the assumption it would be accepted. Later that month, a meeting was held to incorporate the East Yorkshire Aero Company as a limited company, with Neville as the Managing Director and his father as Chairman.

Consequently, a planning application was submitted to the East Riding County Council, which proposed development of parts of the fields on the east side of Staken Road, Preston, south of the Hull to Withernsea railway line for the purposes of a private airfield.

Surprising just about everybody involved, a strong objection was lodged on the 7 September by the Distillers Company, who at the time operated a large factory producing chemicals within the vicinity of the airfield. The objection read as follows:

<u>COPY</u>

THE DISTILLERS COMPANY LIMITED

Chemical Division

Telephone:
Mayfair 8867
Telegrams:
Chemdiv, London, Telex.

Devonshire House,
Mayfair Place,
Piccadilly,
London, W.1.

7th September 1959

The County Planning Officer,
The East Riding County Council,
Town & County Planning Department,
County Hall,
Beverley
E. Yorkshire.

Dear Sir,

We thank you for your letter dated 31st August advising us of the application made by the East Yorkshire Aero Club to establish a flying field adjacent to our works at Salt End, Hedon.

We view this proposal with the gravest concern and oppose it vigorously on the following grounds:-

1. Our Saltend factory has been developed over the years from the early 1920s and the area now developed is approximately 200 acres. In addition we have agreed to lease, for further development in the production of chemicals, an additional area of 60 acres extending to the Hull-Hedon road and hold the option to lease, for similar development, a further 40 acres, extending eastwards and bounded on the northern side by the Hull-Hedon road. The proposed flying field is approximately 600 yards only from our existing northern boundary and approximately 150 yards from our future boundary, the Hull-Hedon road.

Our factory contains many buildings of a height of 60 feet and upwards - this is the general type of building in chemical manufacture and our boiler chimneys and water storage tower are 130 feet and 110 feet respectively. The plant in these buildings is used in the processing of liquids, most of which are highly inflammable, many being more inflammable than petroleum spirit. In addition, we store at various places on the site upwards of 10,000,000 gallons of these highly inflammable solvents, in many cases in bulk storage tanks, some of which contain just under 1,000,000 gallons. The value of our property for fire insurance purpose is £14,500,000 and this will rise as the site develops.

The chemicals produced in our factory are key materials and in a number of cases we are the only source of supply in the United Kingdom; any interruption in supplies would give grave repercussions in many industries.

The factory already employed nearly 2,000 persons and, since the chemical processes are continuous and operate throughout the 24 hours for seven days a week, employees are present at the factory at all times. The number of employees is scheduled to rise appreciably during the next few years as the factory expands.

In our view, the possibility of a flying field within a few hundred yards of such installations cannot be entertained in that it would introduce an extremely serious hazard and the consequences within the factory of an airfield accident, which might elsewhere be minor, could well be a devastating outbreak of fire and explosion, with the consequent danger to the life and limb of our many employees and of the local fire brigades who would be engaged in fire fighting, as well as to the property. In this connection, we have obtained the advice of the Chief Fire Officer of the Hull City Brigade and we understand that he considers the proposal to be a potential hazard which he views with alarm in relation to the nature of the installations at our factory and that his view is supported by the County Chief Fire Officer.

As a further point we should mention that on our plant boundary are the installations of Shell, which consist almost entirely of storage for petroleum. Any hazard which increases the possibility of fire at these installations is also of concern to us, since the possibility of the spread of fire from their premises is a hazard of which we are constantly aware.

2. We note in the letter from the Ministry of Transport and Civil Aviation that "building development adjacent to the West and South boundaries may, if the approaches are not safeguarded, prejudice the declared runway lengths and the size of the manoeuvring area available for use, but it is thought that our licensing standards would not be infringed".

As previously mentioned, our development of the factory is scheduled to extend to the Hull-Hedon road. The extensions are based on the manufacture and storage of chemicals closely integrated around central services which are already established in our existing works. They will follow the lines of our present production and will include tall buildings of the type already in use. Since the northern boundary of these extensions is within 150 yards of the proposed flying field and taking into account the type of installation planned it would seem that the approaches to the field could not be safeguarded and the proposed site for the aerodrome is most unsuitable.

In view of the foregoing we wish to lodge a strong objection to the proposal to establish a flying field north of the Hull-Hedon road and east of Stakes Lane.

If you or your committee should wish any further information we shall be glad to provide this at any time.

Yours faithfully,

For THE DISTILLERS COMPANY LIMITED

(Signed) W.E. Cash

Division Assistant Managing Director

The Distillers Company argued that as their factory had been developed over many years with the potential to be developed further in the future, an informal arrangement was in place so that if future development were to happen, more land could be allocated for the company to use. It just so happened that some of this land overlapped the former Hedon Aerodrome. The company also argued that in the event of an accident, such as if a plane was to come into contact with the factory, the chances of death would be great indeed. This was exacerbated by the fact that there were large storage units at the site containing petroleum and other flammable chemicals. One newspaper described such an event as a potential holocaust. The objection came as a great surprise to the flying club, particularly Neville, who admitted to having no inclination that an objection would be lodged against him. He argued that the Distillers Company had known of the club's activities since 1958 and yet nothing had been raised in that time. The affair eventually reached deadlock, which he was extremely disappointed about.

On the 23 September, a decision was reached by the East Riding Planning Authority Committee, and confirmed by surveyor Mr H.L. Ingham of the Holderness Rural District Council. Mr Ingham confirmed that the letter received from the Distillers Company largely influenced their decision to refuse use of the site for flying. The news was also featured in the Hull Daily Mail two days later. In the article, Neville expressed his disappointment but confirmed that he would appeal the decision. The Hedon Town Council also supported the decision that a flying club might be a nuisance, in view of any future housing and industrial developments taking place.

Top: The works at Saltend. **Bottom**: Saltend, looking westwards. The moored vessel is in the entrance to Hedon Haven. [Courtesy of the Hull Daily Mail]

[Courtesy of the Hull Daily Mail]

Saltend refinery, looking north from the Humber – Hedon Aerodrome is in the centre of the picture, left of the top of the cooling tower. Staithes Road runs on northwards from the dual carriageway approach road to the refinery.

48

Having investigated the matter further, Mr Bilton, solicitor to the aero club sent a letter to the Holderness Rural District Council on the 4 November. In this, it seemed to him clear that the existing use right under Section 12 of the Town and Country Planning Act was applicable to Hedon Aerodrome, particularly as the aerodrome was in use right up to the outbreak of the Second World War, and that aircraft were not removed until well after this in around February 1940. Use of the aerodrome had been approved by the Hull Corporation Planning Committee, and was present in their discussions until around 1948. It had been labelled as such in the Kingston-upon-Hull (South East Hull and District) Town Planning Scheme 1933, which was approved on the 24 March 1933. Thereafter, various applications were made there during 1934 and 1935, which included the erection of a wireless transmitter, a petrol store and a hangar and clubhouse.

Apart from various grazing lettings, temporary tenancies and occupation by various military bodies during the war period, the land had remained unoccupied and in his view, could not have any use other than an aerodrome and flying club. The land had been let for grazing from time to time, with the owners apparently ensuring that the grassland did not deteriorate so as to not lose the existing use rights. Similarly, the land had not been subject to an agricultural tenancy within the Agricultural Holdings Act.

It is thought that the only structural demolition that the airfield had faced was lavatory accommodation by armed forces during the war. The hangar and clubhouse had been substantially unaltered, and the fact that the hangar had continued to exist and not been modified for any other purpose, suggested there would be a valid existing use case for the continued usage of the structure in this way. Additionally, the hangar was only suitable for the storage of aircraft and therefore he argued that it would be useless for the Hull Corporation to argue that it was not a hangar when it clearly was.

The basis of the appeal was relying on Section 12 of the aforementioned Act, with the following points being referenced:

Section 12 (5) (A): Planning permission is not required in the case of land which, on the appointed day (1 July 1948) is being used temporarily for a purpose other than the purpose for which it is normally used, in respect of the resumption of the use of the land for the last mentioned purpose.

Section 12 (5) (C): Planning permission is not required in the case of land which, on the appointed day (1 July 1948) is unoccupied in respect of the use of the land for the purpose which it was last used.

With war being declared on the 3 September 1939, the Air Navigation Order 1939 brought an end to all civilian flying throughout the United Kingdom. The war, in effect, prevented existing use for the duration of the emergency. Additionally, in February 1940, civil aerodromes were requisitioned for war purposes and this included Hedon. These matters further prevented the resumption of the existing use for many years, even after the war, owing to damages incurred during it. The damage was evidently never corrected by either the Air Ministry or the War Department, and this resulted in the herculean task of putting it to rights by the East Yorkshire Aero Club.

Mr Bilton had hoped that this letter would convince the Hull Corporation to agree to the existing use of the aerodrome and flying club, in turn ensuring that both he and the flying club would not have to go down the route of a formal appeal through the planning process. Rather unfortunately, his efforts would prove to have little effect.

In November, it was reported that discussions had taken place between the helicopter operator Fison-Airwork (later to merge with Bristow Helicopters) and the Hull Corporation with regard to the possibility of operating short point-to-point air services to and from the city. Initially, this would be done using helicopters but in time STOL (short take-off and landing) aircraft would also be utilised. A committee were authorised to give the company access to every facility available in the city, as well as ensuring that negotiations relating to the purchase of Sammy's Point as a helicopter base would be accelerated. Mr Bond, operating manager of the company, stated that they would be prepared to base a Hiller 12C helicopter in the city 'almost immediately' and should this prove successful, larger types of helicopter would also be used. Owing to excellent road links, he suggested that Hedon could also satisfy their needs.

DEATH OF AN AIRPORT:

The Hedon Aerodrome Saga

1960

In contrast to the optimism at the turn of 1959, 1960 seemed to offer setback after setback for the newly formed flying club. On the 7 January, Mr H.A. Short, General Manager at the North Eastern Region of British Railways and the British Transport Commission, made contact with the Town Clerk of the Hull Corporation in reference to the telegraph pole issue. In the letter, Mr Short stated that the underground cable which had been laid in 1934, whilst adequate to accommodate the wires of the time, had reached full capacity. Additional cables were required and it was decided that it would be more economical to use overhead poles rather than go underground.

The matter of installing these poles was discussed with a secretary of the flying club only after they had been put up, according to Neville. Despite this, the Ministry of Transport who had previously surveyed the airfield, decided that single-engine machines such as the Tiger Moth could operate with these in place. If twin-engine planes were to be used, then the position would need to be re-evaluated. It was therefore decided that they remain in situ.

On the 16 January, Mr Alston confirmed the communication between the Town Clerk and the British Transport Commission, requesting observations as to the accuracy of their statements. A few days later, Neville supplied Mr Alston with the sequence of events from the flying club's point of view. This was as follows:

1. There was no communication prior to the telegraph poles being installed, which was first noticed by the club on the 21 April 1959. By then, the work was well underway in installing them.
2. A letter was sent on 22 April 1959 from the club to Mr I.G. McGregor, Traffic Manager of British Railways in Hull, and the matter was also reported to Mr Allen at the Guildhall.
3. Mr McGregor called and discussed the situation with the Aero Club on 24 April, stating he would speak with their signals section.
4. A representative of the Ministry of Civil Aviation was informed, who stated the overhead cables would prevent use of a 100 yard width for the full length of the airfield, parallel to the railway for N/S landings or take-offs. Whilst the Ministry would be prepared to license the airfield for single-engine light aircraft, such as a Tiger Moth, the number of runways would need to be reduced because of the restriction imposed by the 100 yard strip along the railway. The cables would also prove to be a hazard to any aircraft landing in poor visibility, and particularly for student pilots.
5. A second interview was conducted with Mr McGregor.

It was hoped that both single-engine and twin-engine aircraft would use the airfield at some point, but Neville believed that the overhead cables would restrict flying of lighter aircraft and probably make the airfield unpopular to potential members and aircraft owners. The fact that twin-engine aircraft would be completely barred from use would only result in a further lack of support from those wishing to use the airfield. He argued that when the airfield and flying club were formed, a great deal of local publicity was generated and he found it hard to believe that British Railways were unaware of the club's existence. Apparently the workmen installing the poles knew all about it.

53

An appeal, lodged by the East Yorkshire Aero Club against the planning refusal from the previous year, was to be held at The Guildhall in Hull, the headquarters of the Hull Corporation, on the 10 February. A number of people were lined up in support of the club, with the appeal notification reading as follows:

```
THE EAST YORKSHIRE AERO CLUB LIMITED (1) AGAINST THE
REFUSAL OF THE HOLDERNESS RURAL DISTRICT COUNCIL
ACTING ON BEHALF OF THE LOCAL PLANNING AUTHORITY TO
PERMIT A FLYING FIELD FOR AERO CLUB, ERECTION OF A NEW
LADIES TOILETS ON SITE OF OLD TOILETS, HANGAR FOR
STORAGE OF AIRCRAFT USE AS A STORE AND OFFICE, AND A
CLUBHOUSE FOR USE ON THIS SITE AT HEDON AERODROME. (2)
AGAINST THE DETERMINATION BY HOLDERNESS RURAL DISTRICT
COUNCIL UNDER SECTION D OF THE TOWN AND COUNTRY
PLANNING ACT, 1947 REGARDING THE PROPOSED DEVELOPMENT
OF THIS SITE.
```

Mr Hullock, the Ministry of Civil Aviation surveyor who had first inspected the field in July/August 1953 and again in the summer of 1959 following the installation of telegraph poles, originally did not feel it necessary for him to attend the appeal. According to Neville, his reasons were that as the Ministry had already issued a licence for the airfield, all existing hazards had been taken into account for daytime flying. Days later however, Mr Hullock was confirmed to be attending it, having had a change of heart at the last minute. On the 6 February, a map of the Hedon Aerodrome site was drawn up, which included markings for the areas leased by the Distillers Company, Hull Speedways Ltd, The Territorial Army Association, the area licensed to The Secretary of State for Air, and the boundary of the area leased to the club.

54

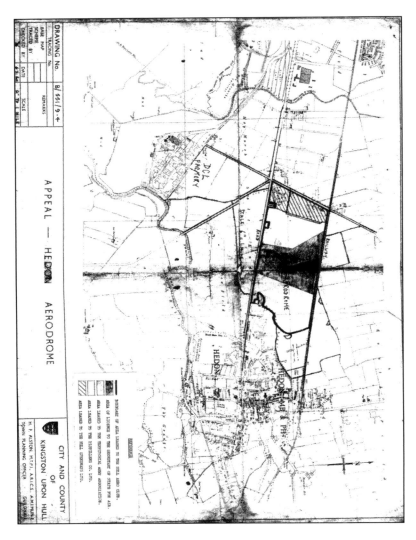

A plan of the Hedon Aerodrome site, prepared for the appeal by the Hull
Corporation, 6 February 1960

The day before the appeal, evidence including a brief history of tenancies and reasons for the refusal was submitted by the Town Planning Officer at the Hull Corporation, Mr Alston. The evidence read as follows:

CITY AND COUNTY OF KINGSTON UPON HULL
HEDON AERODROME

Evidence of Harold Fielding Alston, M.T.P.I., A.R.I.C.S., A.M.I.MUN.E., Town Planning Officer, Kingston upon Hull.

- - - - - - - -

The appeal is on two counts, first against the determination under Section 17 of the Town and Country Planning Act, 1947 that planning permission is required for the use of the land on the north side of Hedon Road as a private airfield and the erection of a lavatory block, and secondly against the planning refusal for use of the land for this purpose.

With regard to the Section 17 determination it is considered that the site has an existing use as an aerodrome for the following reasons. The site was developed as an airfield in 1929 and leased to National Flying Services Ltd. in October, 1929, who used it until March 1934. In the Kingston upon Hull (South East Hull District) Town Planning Scheme, 1933, the site was shown as an Aerodrome (white edged green), this scheme being in operation until 1.7.1948. Immediately thereafter the site was leased to Hull Aero Club, who continued to use the site together with other commercial airlines, as an aerodrome, until February, 1940. During this period from 1929 to 1940 the land was also used for grazing purposes.

During the period December, 1940, to September, 1947, 51 acres of the site together with the hangars was requisitioned by the Secretary of State for War, and the Secretary of State for Air was in occupation of 69 acres with a Licence to glide from the site. In October, 1947, part of the site was leased for a period to Hull Speedways Ltd., as a motorcycle speedway track, this use terminated in September, 1949. In May, 1952, part of the site was leased for a term of years to the Territorial Army

Association. These uses being indicated on Plan B/551/9-4 now submitted. During the whole of the period since the war the site has also continued to be let, as in the case of pre-war, for short term grazing tenancies.

-2-

A list of all tenancies since 1929 is submitted herewith. The cultivation of 26 acres during and immediately after the war was done under direction from the Ministry of Agriculture under war-time emergency powers.

From the above it is apparent that the site was used as an airfield for a considerable period after 7th January, 1937, and that this use was terminated due to the war. Subsequently the site has either been under requisition or the subject of temporary uses. It is considered, therefore, that the existing use for the purposes of Section 12 (5) of the Town and Country Planning Act, 1947 remains an airfield.

Extracts from the minutes of the Aerodrome Committee are submitted herewith, indicating the Corporation's intentions and efforts during the post-war period, to re-establish flying from Hedon Aerodrome. The early efforts were unsuccessful due to the type of aircraft then envisaged but recently discussions have taken place with a major company which indicate that the site would be ideal for STOL (short take-off and landing) aircraft and that this is the type likely to come into use for inter-City services.

MLH/JAF.12.
9th February, 1960.

-3-

Planning permission for the use of the site as a private airfield was refused "on the ground that flying from the airfield would involve danger to adjacent industrial undertakings". The Local Planning Authority have stated that it was with some regret that planning permission was refused and that in coming to their decision they were influenced by the objections raised by The Distillers Company Limited. The

Minister of Local Government and Planning in circular 58/51, drew the attention of Local Planning Authorities to the fact that they should not attempt to control under planning powers, matters dealt with under other legislation and that planning should not be used as a universal long stop. There would appear to be no reason for refusal on planning grounds but that in view of objections raised permission has been refused contrary to the Minister's direction in the above circular. The relevant powers in this case would appear to be held by the Minister of Civil Aviation under the Air Navigation Order, 1954 and the Air Navigation General Regulations, 1954. In a letter dated 8th August, 1959, his Regional Controller has stated that taking into account the existing and proposed development in the area and other factors, they were not sufficient to prejudice the issue of an aerodrome licence.

Objections were also raised by the British Transport Commission in respect of land in their ownership on the south side of Hedon Road and in this connection it is pointed out that only the land to the south west of Paull Road is zoned for industrial development in the East Riding County Development Plan. This land is shown on Drawing No. B/551/9-3.

It is understood that the Ministry of Civil Aviation requirements for the type of aircraft envisaged are one main runway 100 yards wide by 700 yds. long and one or more secondary runways of the same width and 600 yds. long, free from obstructions to an angle of 1 in 7 at the sides and 1 in 20 at both ends. Drawing No. B/551/9-3 now submitted, shows that the main existing buildings of The Distillers Co. Ltd. are some 4,000 ft. from the end of the nearest runway and in any case are not on the line of approach to Co. Ltd. were in existence when the site was used by the Hull Aero Club and but for the intervention of the war, the site would have continued to be used for flying purposes. With regard to the land zoned for industrial purposes, the nearest point is approximately 1,400 ft. from the end of a runway, and this would allow for clearance of obstructions 70 ft. high. The effect on the remaining land owned by the British Transport Commission is also shown and is not considered as likely to have any marked effect on its development if subsequently zoned for industrial purposes. It is also pointed out that both Shell Mex and B.P. Ltd. and Esso Petroleum Co. have substantial installations at Salt End in the immediate vicinity of The Distillers Co. Ltd., but neither company have raised any objection to the proposal. Certain telegraph poles along the northern boundary of the site, on land owned by the British Transport Commission, represent, at the present time, an obstruction to flying. Discussions are, however, in hand which are likely to lead to an agreement for the removal of these poles.

In view of the foregoing it is considered, first that the site has an existing use as an Aerodrome; secondly that the grounds of refusal are not planning matters, being better and more specifically controlled by other legislation and thirdly that in any case the grounds of refusal are unreasonable in the circumstances.

The inquiry was held over three days from the 10-12 February. News coverage was extensive throughout, with numerous reports being published in the local press. One such report, published on the 10 February entitled 'Hedon Airfield Ban: Appeal', revealed how Mr G. Styles, representing the Hull Corporation, had argued that as the owners of the land, the Corporation were more concerned with the question of determination. He had contended that the County Planning Authority's decision was improper and based on inaccurate information. 'To say that the use of the airport had been discontinued does not mean that there was no intention ever to resume that use… it does not mean that the use had been extinguished,' he argued. Mr Alston had also submitted considerable evidence during the case, taken from the Hull Aerodrome Committee minutes which, he said, indicated the Corporation's intention and efforts during the post-war period to re-establish flying from the airfield.

Although discussions had taken place about alternative uses, the Hull Corporation apparently had at no time decided to abandon the use of Hedon airfield for flying purposes. Mr Styles added that serious discussions had recently taken place with airline operators concerning the use of the airfield by STOL (short take-off and landing) aircraft, the type of aircraft then used by airlines. Throughout the Inquiry, the flying club was represented by Mr S. G. Davies, whilst the East Riding County Council was represented by Mr W. F. Hodgson. Mr J. F. Cobb acted as representative for the British Transport Commission and The Distillers Company, whilst Councillor N. Simpson also attended as a representative of the Holderness Rural District Council.

The following day, an article entitled 'Airfield fears are born of ignorance' was published, revealing how Mr Davies had suggested that the East Riding County Council did not have the 'faintest idea' of the true factors involved when they refused the planning permission submitted by the flying club. He stated that there had been a lot of prejudice against flying, and suggested that a single aircraft crash would make the news but '1,000 car crashes' would not. He further went on to add that 'popular mistrust, as is so often the case is born of ignorance. I think the fact that there is a great deal of ignorance among the parties here today has already become apparent.'

Referring to earlier statements made by the Distillers Company representative Mr Cobb on the danger of low flying aircraft, Mr Davies suggested that he had 'already attempted to make (their) blood run cold with stories of fatal accidents at Hedon in the thirties' and that these 'must be placed in their proper perspective'. 'They happened twenty-five years ago... half the history of aviation. Aircraft of the sixties differ radically from aircraft of the thirties', highlighting how there were now rigorous checks on both the pilots and their machines. Mr Davies had also expressed surprise that two neighbouring petroleum companies, Shell Mex-BP and Esso Petroleum who also had substantial installations in the immediate vicinity of the Distillers Company's works, had not similarly complained. Considering the crux of the Distillers Company argument was that a fire in one of their installations might hazard their installations also; 'they surely were the best judges' he stated.

That same day, another article entitled 'Runways "Pointed at Heart of Hedon" ', was printed, highlighting the apparent anxiety felt by the people of Hedon regarding the proposed airfield. Statements by Councillor N. Simpson, a representative of the Holderness Rural District Council, included how there were fears that the airfield would 'point straight at the heart of (the) town like a pistol'. Mr Styles argued however that the resumption of flying at Hedon did not require planning approval by the East Riding Council, and the intention of reopening it had never been abandoned. Were it not for the war, he suggested, the site would still be used. Mr Hodgson stated that the Distillers Company were highly troubled about the risks involved.

Rival newspaper The Yorkshire Post had also picked up the story and the following day published an article entitled 'Airfield seen as danger to factory – Secret drugs made there'. During the appeal, the Manager of the Distillers Company Mr John Howlett suggested that the supplies of 'secret drugs' being exported to China, used to help manage the effects of tuberculosis, could be affected as a result of a fire or explosion at his factory. He stated that they were the only company in the country manufacturing these drugs, and the dangers would 'be increased' if a flying club were allowed to use the nearby land as an airfield. He was questioned by Mr Cobb, who was also representing the works, about whether a fire or explosion would amount to a 'national disaster' and Mr Howlett revealed that the finished product was currently being stored in tanks and drums on the premises, which at any one time exceeded five million gallons.

The value of fire insurance for the factory was at £21 million, with around 2 million tons of petroleum processed at the factories in 1958. The consequences of an aircraft accident, either there or at a neighbouring installation, could potentially result in a 'devastating outbreak of fire and explosion and result in the loss of life of many company employees'. An estate surveyor to the British Transport Commission, Mr Henry Littlefair, also referred to the installations which handled millions of gallons of inflammable material. If there were an aircraft accident, he stated, it could 'without exaggeration amount to a holocaust involving the loss of many lives, as well as property'. His comments would be seized on by the Hull Daily Mail, who the following day published the headline 'Flying Accident could cause Saltend Holocaust'.

With the inquiry coming to a close, Mr Cobb further suggested that the Hull Corporation were using the flying club's application as 'the thin end of the wedge' to reopen the Hedon airfield for commercial flying. 'Sooner or later, there would be bound to be an accident. Any damage to the company would be damage to the nation, because they are such vast exporters.' On the 12 February, the inquiry closed.

A selection of the articles published during the Inquiry, highlighting the flurry of interest in the case, 10-12 February 1960.

The Inspector conducting the two day inquiry, Mr A. Chown of the Ministry of Housing and Local Government, visited the airfield at Hedon on the 12 February, accompanied by the representatives of the parties concerned. His purpose was to inspect the eighty-acre aerodrome as well as the hangar, and he was greeted by Neville's Tiger Moth aeroplane that had been stripped down for inspection and maintenance. Interestingly, Mr Chown had inspected the aerodrome some thirty years prior in 1929, when the site was to be used as a municipal airport. The final decision was to be made by the Minister of Housing and Local Government, acting on Mr Chown's recommendations.

Mr Chown inspecting the Hedon Aerodrome hangar, Neville and his Tiger Moth aeroplane can also be seen, 12 February 1960.

Following the three-day inquiry, an eighteen-page report was drafted and completed by the inspector on the 26 February. Within the report, sections included information about the site and surroundings, the case for the Hull Corporation, the case for the appellants, evidence submitted by the Ministry of Aviation, the case for the local planning authority, the case for the Distillers Company and the Transport Commission, as well as the inspector's own conclusions and recommendations. Notable extracts from the report included:

THE CASE FOR HULL CORPORATION

20.   The extracts from the minutes of the Aerodrome Committee indicated the Corporation's intentions and efforts during the post-war period to re-establish flying from Hedon Aerodrome. The early efforts were unsuccessful due to the type of recent discussions that had taken place with a major company which indicated that the site would be ideal for short take-off and landing aircraft which were likely to come into use for inter-city services.

21.   From 1929 onwards the aerodrome committee, and afterwards the town planning committee, had used the land for flying purposes or tried to get flying resumed on the land. At no time had the committee decided to abandon the land as an airfield. They had certainly had discussions about other sites when they had thought they would require a larger airport or when they were discussing the possibility of helicopters. But at no time had they decided on another site either within or outside the city.

29.   It was agreed that the main landing strip pointed towards the town of Hedon, but it was maintained, that by the time aircraft got over the town they would be at a considerable height and, in any case, the planes were light aircraft and the noise would not be anywhere near intolerable, as the planes were neither jets nor helicopters. It was maintained that because the Air Ministry wanted the airport shifted to Neat Marsh it did not mean that Hedon airfield was no longer suitable as an airport because Air Ministry and civil flying requirements were entirely different.

38.   Neither Shell-Mex and B.P. Limited nor Esso Petroleum Company had raised any objection to the proposal although they had substantial installations at Salt End in the immediate vicinity of the Distillers Company. Telegraph poles along the railway line to the north of the site were obstructions to flying but discussions were in hand which would lead to an agreement for a removal of these poles.

40.   It was agreed that the corporation had been taken by surprise to hear that land to the south of Hedon Road was to be developed for industrial purposes. It was not shown for this purpose on the county development plan, the corporation had not

been consulted nor had the matter been brought before the joint consultative committee.

CASE FOR THE APPELLANTS

44. The appellants had a difficult case because they had to establish the negative, that what they proposed was not dangerous. But a planning permission ought to be granted unless there were good reasons for refusal and therefore it was up to the local planning authority to establish that there was a danger. There was no evidence of danger; certain people were apprehensive of danger, but this was a different thing from establishing that a danger existed. The appellants had a popular prejudice against aircraft to overcome; if one aircraft crashed it was reported in the newspapers but if a thousand cars crashed they were not reported.

45. The county council spoke of their experience with other aerodromes and mentioned the figure of 4,500 feet clearance from the end of the runways. No statutory directions mentioned this figure and the county council must be thinking in terms of commercial passenger and freight planes and it showed that the county council in fact had no idea of the technical implications of the application.

49. The aircraft which it was proposed to fly had a very steep rate of ascent and flew at low speeds. It was almost beyond possibility that such an aircraft, in whatever difficulty, could not and would not avoid the surrounding villages, the borough of Hedon and the Hull-Hedon road. The appellants' intention was to keep to light aircraft and the field was not and never could be suitable for heavier aircraft because of the limited runways available.

51. The Distillers Company admitted that during the 1930s flying took place from the airfield without any incident involving either the Distillers Company Limited or any other installation at Salt End.

53. The fact the Ministry of Aviation had indicated their willingness to grant a licence showed that there was no danger to any installation or property in the neighbourhood. Pilots of

light aircraft, by their training, avoided flying over developed areas and there were ample uncoloured and undeveloped areas in the immediate vicinity of the proposed airfield to allow the continuation of this practice.

54.   Undue weight was given by the local planning authority to certain representations made to it without the accuracy of them being examined. It was understood that the statement attributed to the chief fire officer of the Hull City Fire Brigade was not made by him.

56.   The amenities of Hull would be improved by the existence of an airfield near Hedon. The site was suitable for an airfield and it was the only such site within easy distance of Hull. The aerodrome was four miles from the centre of Hull and close to a main road which led directly to the centre of the city. There was no other flying field having facilities for club flying within fifty miles by road from Hull.

A witness from the Ministry of Aviation gave the following evidence

66.   The surrounding residential and industrial areas were too far distant for any danger or nuisance to result because of the angles of climb and descent which club type aeroplanes had. The distance from the road to the proposed edge of the landing area was sufficient to ensure safe clearance of the traffic by these aircraft.

8.   In relation particularly to the Distillers Company's installation there was no need for anyone to fly over it, the airfield and landing strips were so disposed as to provide unrestricted use without doing this. All licensed airfields were listed by the Ministry in the U.K. Air Pilot and it was customary to list significant features within three miles of the field.

73.   It was open to the Distillers Company to have an entry made in the U.K. Air Pilot if they thought that aircraft should not fly over their factory and this would be made in the remarks column which dealt with local rules and advice to visitors.

76.   It was agreed that an official inspection for a licence had not been made as in fact no application for a licence had been made, nor had nearby premises been visited. It was agreed that he had not considered Section 40 of the Civil Aviation Act, 1949, nor the extent of damage that might occur, but he considered that satisfactory flights could be made from the airfield off the line of development. It was agreed that the factories had not been visited, nor had inquiries been made about the membership of the club, but it was agreed that there would be learner pilots. The Ministry would specify which type of aircraft the strips were suitable for and the licence would limit the use of the airfield to daytime and there would have to be adequate fire and rescue facilities on the site.

This was the end of the Minister of Aviation official's evidence and examination

77.   It was submitted that the Ministry of Aviation's licences were given annually and new development near the airfield could be taken into consideration each year before the issue of a licence. The expert witness had said that the airfield was safe for the club aircraft now, planning permission ought therefore to be given now and the future would be controlled by the annual licences which were ultimately a much more effective means of control. If it were felt that more land was needed for the airfield this could be got with the agreement of the corporation. Planning permission had to be obtained first so that the Ministry of Aviation did not waste its time issuing licences to airfields which were likely to be refused permission on planning grounds.

CASE FOR THE LOCAL PLANNING AUTHORITY

As to the refusal of planning permission

100.   Adverse comments on the proposal were received from the Distillers Company Limited and from the British Transport Commission. Shell Mex replied that they had no objection to the proposal so long as it did not in any way influence the local planning authority's decision when they put forward proposals for erecting further petroleum storage tanks. Esso Petroleum had no objection but stipulated that should warning lights be necessary

at the top of their tanks or elevated structures they would expect the club or the Ministry of Transport to bear the cost.

104. The situation which existed in 1929 when the Hull aerodrome was first opened had been radically altered by the development of great new industries at Salt End and the old Hedon racecourse could not now be regarded as a suitable place for an airfield.

106. It was agreed that the use of the airfield by light aircraft might not create much danger but that its use by inter-city aircraft would. The local planning authority considered that the airfield would be a bad neighbour to an industrial site and in their opinion industry was the more important of the two uses which had to be considered.

THE CASE FOR THE DISTILLERS COMPANY LIMITED AND THE TRANSPORT COMMISSION

108. The British Transport Commission strongly supported the decision of the local planning authority to refuse permission for the proposed airfield on the grounds that flying from the airfield would involve danger to adjacent undertakings. The Commission had at Salt End jetty facilities for berthing and discharge of petrol tankers; the activities of their lessees included the bulk storage of petrol and chemical manufacture involving the use of highly inflammable and dangerous chemicals. The commission owned the Salt End Estate, part of it was allocated for industrial purposes on the county development plan and the remainder was the subject of an assurance given by the county clerk that any application for the development of the land would be considered on its merits and would not be refused permission merely on the ground that it was not allocated for industrial purposes on the development plan.

109. The commission were constructing a new jetty capable of taking tankers carrying 18,000 tons. The prevailing wind blew off the river from the south-west and aircraft taking off from the proposed airfield would fly in the general direction of the commission's developed land. Shell Mex had permission to extend on the west of Salt End Lane right up to the Hull-Hedon road. Similarly, the Distillers Company had permission to extend up to the Hull-Hedon road to the south-east of Salt End Lane and south-west of Paull Road. The Distillers Company were planning to

extend to the north-east side of Paull Road and the local planning authority had forwarded this proposal to the Minister with a recommendation that the proposal should be favourably considered. The effect of all this would be to bring the industrial land within 340 yards of the nearest point of the airfield and eventually to within 170 yards.

110. The presence of the airfield so close to these installations would create a serious risk of extensive and disastrous damage from what might in other areas be a minor flying accident. Many accidents occurred at landing or take off, regulating conditions might on occasions not be adhered to, and the effect of this would be a holocaust involving the loss of many lives as well as destruction of property.

115. Many of the products were highly inflammable and dangerous. Stocks of finished products and raw materials held at the factory at any one time exceeded 5 million tons and considerable attention had been paid to safety precautions and fire prevention. Special precautions were taken to store the products under the right conditions, the strictest regulations were in force to prevent ignition and a nitrogen cover was provided to all tanks wherever practicable. There was direct communication with the Hull City Fire Brigade and in the event of a fire alarm being pressed in any part of the factory the city fire brigade despatched a major turn-out of fire fighting machines. There was a continuous shift rota of security officers who collected all matches and lighters from people entering the factory and who patrolled the factory day and night. The penalty for carrying matches or lighters or for smoking was instant dismissal. Acetylene, which was a highly dangerous gas liable to explosion under uncontrolled conditions, was generated in the factory.

120. It was submitted on behalf of the Transport Commission and the Distillers Company that the local planning authorities were well within their rights to take into account the safety of property and persons on the land around the airfield. The evidence given by the Ministry of Aviation representative showed that he was concerned solely with the safety of the aircraft and that he had considered that solely in relation to the existing development. He had assumed that Austere and Tiger Moths were going to be used, but he had been the only witness for the appellants, no one had come forward from the club to say what

aircraft were going to be used, what proportion of learners there were going to be or what the insurance arrangements against accidents were. The corporation could have produced an expert witness in the person of the chief fire officer but they had not done so and the statement attributed to the chief fire officer by the appellant should be ignored. The corporation's interest in this case was obviously in that they regarded this application as the thin end of the wedge and they saw a chance to get Hedon airport going again, but the results of a busy airport in this situation would be appalling. The three accidents which had taken place before the war were in areas which were now developed. A plane could equally fall in the Distillers Company factory. It was an appalling risk to take with immature flyers; it could damage the nation industrially and result in much loss of life.

On the Section 1 determination it was submitted on behalf of the Transport Commission and the Distillers Company

122. It was clearly not the intention of the corporation to continue to use Hedon as an airfield when in July, 1939 they were looking at Neat Marsh as a possible site for an airfield. Whatever K.L.M. may have said in their letter about the cause of missing out Hull on their flights, it was obvious that by 1939 the Hedon airfield had reached the end of its usefulness either because of fog or because of the limited size of the runways. The post-war minutes of the committees concerned with the aerodrome site showed quite clearly that they were intent on finding any tenant other than one who wanted to operate the field as an aerodrome.

INSPECTOR'S CONCLUSIONS

On the Section 17 determination

127. The resolution of the aerodrome committee on 12th June, 1947, to take no further action on the two applications for the use of the land for flying because of the motor cycle and horse racing which was proposed on the site, clearly shows that the

corporation had abandoned the idea of using the land for flying. The transfer of the site from the aerodrome committee to the town planning committee, the lapse of the subscription to the Aerodrome Owners' Association and the representations made at the development plan inquiry to have the land shown as industrial are further proof that the corporation had abandoned the idea of keeping the land as a municipal airport. I consider that there was a complete break in the intention of keeping this land for flying from 1947 to 1959 when interest started again because of this application and the possibility of using short take-off and landing craft made it appear that the old airfield could again be used for intercity planes. During this period the hangar remained out off from the airfield by banking of the speedway track and in my view the grazing which, except on the speedway track for two years, was carried on over the whole site was a use in its own right despite the less-than-a-year tenancies, and it was not carried on because it was hoped that the eventual use of the land would be for flying.

On the refusal of planning permission

128. In my view, if planning permission is required, there is a strong objection to the use of the appeal site for club flying because of the danger to the Salt End industries, principally to the factory of the Distillers Company Limited. The small size of the planes and their steep rate of climb and descent would, in my opinion, prevent them from damaging the amenities of the surrounding communities. The licensing by the Ministry of Aviation would make sure that the field would be safe from the flying point of view in the matters of size of field and freedom from surrounding obstruction.

129. I consider however that the airfield would be a bad neighbour to the industries and that the fears expressed by these industries are fully justified. The industries at present cover an arc of 90° from the centre of the field and they are not very far away in the direction of the prevailing wind and they would be in an area where accidents are liable to happen. The most vulnerable of the sites, the Distillers Company Limited, covers 100 acres and I do not consider that this addition to the already

considerable fire risk can be justified on the need for a flying club on this particular site.

130. The appellants the British Transport Commission and the Distillers Company asked for costs but I do not consider that the circumstances justify awarding them.

<u>INSPECTOR'S RECOMMENDATION</u>

131. I recommend that the appeal should be dismissed on the ground that the use of the appeal site as an airfield for a flying club would mean an unjustifiable increase in the fire risk at the Salt End industries, especially at the factory of the Distillers Company Limited.

During the inquiry, the Hull City Council had publicly protested against the East Riding County Council, who they stated had delayed supplying reasons for their refusal of the flying club. Mr G. Styles, a Solicitor to the Hull Corporation, was quoted in a newspaper article as saying the County Council had supplied them with the necessary information just five days prior to the case taking place. This, inevitably, had not given them sufficient time to rebut any 'misleading and inaccurate' statements made. In any event, Mr Styles suggested that the whole question of planning permission should be ignored, as the Hull Corporation had never actually 'abandoned' the aerodrome. Regardless, it would not be for another eight months until a decision would be reached by the Ministry of Housing and Local Government, and during this time, Neville, his father and the other directors of the East Yorkshire Aero Company fearlessly carried on operations.

On the 11 March, both Neville and his father had visited City Treasurer Mr Pollard C.B.E. to discuss the grazing rights for the summer of the previous year. The following week, Mr Pollard received a telephone call from the farmer, Mr Smith, and on the discussion of payment he agreed to offer the higher sum of £200. That summer, Mr Smith had been given a greater use of the land than originally anticipated, as a consequence of the lack of use by the club. On the 13 April the club accepted the offer, which was agreed in writing on the 13 May.

It was to be a long, arduous wait for the flying club until a decision was reached regarding their appeal. During this time, the club became rather frustrated about the lack of action taking place, making their feelings known to the various powers that be. The fact that interest was still shown towards them by pilots did not help matters, with one such request being made in May by a pilot hoping to visit Hull from Kent using a Chipmunk aircraft. By July, the club, frustrated over the long delays and greatly concerned due to the amount of money which had been put into the project, complained to the Hull Corporation. Concerns about diminishing interest were also put forward, as a result of the lack of activity. The club therefore kindly asked the Hull Corporation to 'hurry up' the Ministry of Housing and Local Government for a decision. It could not come quickly enough.

On the 12 July, the Town Clerk responded to the club's concerns, personally writing to the Ministry asking for a decision to be 'expedited'. On the 20 July, Mr E.W. Porteous of the Ministry responded, stating that he could not give a decision there and then, but that one would be made known as soon as possible. A note at the bottom of the letter, added later on the 20 September shows that Neville had telephoned Mr Porteous about this matter, but again Mr Porteous could not give a date on when a decision was to be expected, describing the case as 'difficult'.

An assistant secretary to the Ministry, Mr G.R. Coles, wrote to Neville on the 21 September following on from his call to Mr Porteous. Despite the matter being of 'considerable importance', he apologised for the delays which were apparently somewhat complicated. A firm date could not be given as to when the appeal would be resolved, but Mr Coles estimated a decision would be made in around three to four weeks. A month later, there were further delays when Mr Coles confirmed that the matter had been postponed again for unknown reasons.

A decision was finally reached on the 28 October, and whilst the wait was over for the club, rather unfortunately for them their appeal was thrown out. The Minister stated that the decision was largely based on the increase of fire risk at the neighbouring factories, judging the airfield as a 'bad neighbour' towards them. In his view, the fears of the Distillers Company were fully justified. Regardless of this, it was to be the end of a long battle for the small flying club, with all hopes of flying from the former aerodrome now extinguished. Unable to afford the costs of taking the matter to the High Court, the East Yorkshire Aero Company fearlessly carried on their operations.

Disagreeing with the decision, Neville believed that in an effort to undermine the support the representative from the Ministry of Aviation had given to the club, the representative had been 'got at' by the Town and County Planning people at Whitehall. He felt the refusal of planning permission was based on 'a few weak excuses', arguing that there was no valid reason as to why the flying club could not continue for another five to ten years. His hopes of forming a municipal airport for the city of Hull continued, and in November he informed the Association of British Aero Clubs and Centres of the situation. Wishing to maintain the club's affiliation with them, he stated that they were looking for an alternative site regardless if there were no guarantees of finding one.

Discussions continued and on the 14 December, Neville made his thoughts known in a letter to Mr G. Miles of the Association. He admitted to wrongly assuming the case 'was in the bag', but felt that the Hull Corporation were supportive of the club throughout the appeal. On reflection, he had underestimated the opposition and overestimated the justice administered from Whitehall themselves. On the surface, non-local people (such as those from Whitehall) might consider the decision made from the evidence available as fair;

however as a Hull native, he felt that some of the evidence supplied by the opposition was 'incomprehensible'. He argued that a local person would know that Councillor Simpson, who had given evidence on behalf of the people of Hedon, was also employed as a security officer by the Distillers Company themselves.

In this highly critical letter, Neville suggested that facts had been distorted by the East Riding Planning Officer, with a judgement being made knowing nothing of local conditions. Instead, facts from the opposition were blindly accepted and he believed that there had been an 'almighty hurry' in getting the case over with. He suggested that practically all of the big industrial companies in Hull supported the idea of a local air terminal, with the exception of the objecting party.

Throughout the previous eighteen months, several executive aircraft had used the field, including his Tiger Moth. He therefore found it strange that Esso and Shell, notable petroleum distributers based at the site, had not opposed the scheme alongside the Distillers Company. Regardless, the letter was likely the result of bitter disappointment after what seemed to be a lot of effort with no payoff. Two days later, he wrote to the Ministry of Aviation describing the decision as a 'miscarriage of justice' and being extremely shocked by it.

On the 17 December, the City Treasurer of the Hull Corporation wrote to Neville in respect of the club's renting of the Hedon Aerodrome land. With an outstanding balance of £500, the Treasurer assumed that the club were no longer interested in renting the field, following the appeal result. The Corporation also had plans to let the land to a farmer the following summer. Annual rent at £350 initially resulted in a balance of £700 overall, but a remittance of £200 made by the sub-letting tenant, Mr Smith, left a balance of £500.

A further remittance due to the ongoing case, the lack of usage by the club and the farmer's continued usage throughout this period was made, leaving £386 in total. In response, Neville's father Albert urged the Corporation to fight the decision, disagreeing with the charge for land which had not been used for flying. He felt that through no fault of its own, the club had been placed in a position where they could not operate or advertise membership and as a result of this there had been no income.

Provisional estimates suggested that around £1,000 had been spent in legal costs for the Hedon project by the East Yorkshire Aero Company. Therefore, the decision to refuse flying was seen as a tragedy for the club and it had been hoped by all involved that the following year would bring some good fortune.

DEATH OF AN AIRPORT:

The Hedon Aerodrome Saga

1961

By January 1961, correspondence had resumed with the Ministry of Aviation and the Town Planning Officer of the Hull Corporation. Neville confirmed the issue of use of Hedon Aerodrome land by the club had been taken up at Ministerial level by the Association of British Aero Clubs and Centres, in tandem with his own contact with the Ministry.

He requested that the Corporation allow sufficient time for the club to fight back on these issues before reserving the land to another party. From his research, he could find no other site like Hedon within four miles of the city of Hull, apart from a small plot in the Neat Marsh area WNW of Preston village. As the site was undeveloped, however, it would be very costly to develop and lacked the suitable road links. He was also negotiating for a flying site around seventeen miles from Hull and suggested that, providing planning permission was obtained, this could be suitable as an alternative for the aero club. In his opinion, seventeen miles would be far too remote for a city airport and because of this, he urged the Corporation to hold on to the Hedon Aerodrome site for them until the matter had been clarified by the Ministry of Aviation and Ministry of Housing and Local Government.

On the 3 February, City Treasurer Mr Pollard responded to the letter, stating that whilst the Corporation would make no demand for rent during 1959 and 1960, he suggested that little could be done in terms of the appeal decision, which the Corporation viewed as final. In a letter to the Ministry of Aviation dated 10 February, Neville did not feel that the Ministry of Housing and Local Government (who oversaw the appeal at Whitehall) possessed the same attitude about the matter as the Ministry of Aviation had. He could not understand why the Ministry of Housing and Local Government, who he felt were inexperienced in dealing with aviation, had settled the matter. As there were no developments about to take place on the airfield, a case regarding the operation of aircraft should have been overseen by the Ministry of Aviation instead, he argued.

On the 21 March, Neville reminded the Corporation that the Ministry of Aviation still considered the site fit for licensing as an airfield and that the result of the appeal made no difference in their support of this. He stated that enquiries were still incoming for use of Hedon as a landing site, with Fenners having recently used it to fly in from Newcastle. Following this, they had expressed an interest in using it again in the future. The engineering company Priestman Brothers were also keen on using the site for executive aircraft, with additional support forthcoming from municipal airports in Yeadon and Newcastle. Both airports had been looking to collaborate with the flying club. Additionally, after inspecting the site for use with STOL Twin Pioneer aircraft, Fisons also deemed it suitable for use by them.

Further correspondence was sent to the Town Planning Officer on the 1 May, suggesting that potential interest in the former RAF aerodrome at Hutton Cranswick for use as an airfield had stalled due to a change in the landowner's mind. Neville also revealed how, that weekend, he had attended an event in Coventry with some flying colleagues, discovering that the town had its own civic aerodrome with plans being put forward for further development. All of the aircraft on display that weekend could be operated from Hedon, he suggested, including the Dornier, which he found could operate in little over fifty yards and could remain airborne with only twenty knots on the air speed indicator. His view of the exhibition was that it showed air development was advancing at a 'startling rate', particularly in terms of light passenger and executive aircraft.

Whilst at the show, Neville had lengthy discussions with the Chairman for the Association of British Aero Clubs and Centres regarding Hedon. He assured him that the issue of the former airport would be brought up at their next meeting the following week. Neville had also managed to arrange an interview with the Ministry of Aviation; however he was advised by the Chairman that it would be best if, during this meeting, he was accompanied by one or more Hull Members of Parliament.

As the Ministry of Housing and Local Government had already made their decision regarding the future of the airfield, Mr Alston doubted whether anything positive could be achieved by pursuing the matter further. He stated that the Corporation were considering the future of air services in the city and that it was quite possible they were going to approach the Ministry themselves. He felt that it would 'rather duplicate matters' if Neville were to contact them as well.

On the 11 May, Neville dispatched a letter to the then Member of Parliament for Hull North, Mr Coulson, informing him of the matter relating to the Hedon airfield. He informed Mr Coulson of his difficulties in persuading the Hull Corporation that the matter was worth pursuing and stated he was still awaiting an outcome regarding his enquiries to the Ministry of Aviation. An interview with them had been arranged, in which he would be accompanied by the Chairman of the Association of British Aero Clubs and Centres. Frustrated about the 'intolerable' position that Hull was in without an air terminal, he requested to speak with him at his soonest convenience.

From recent research, he had been able to determine a more accurate picture of the airfield's background, including information apparently proving that the Hedon site had not been disregarded as a future airfield, contrary to what was claimed by the Ministry of Housing and Local Government. He also had reason to believe that the Corporation were now willing to use Hedon themselves. On the 16 May, Mr Coulson's private secretary invited Neville to chat with him whilst he was meeting with the Ministry of Aviation in London.

An article published in the Hull Daily Mail entitled 'Hull Bid for Airport', reported how a Hull Town Planning Committee meeting had taken place with a view to finding a suitable airport for the city. The committee, keen to find out the Ministry's policy on civil aerodromes, were reminded by the Town Planning Officer Mr Alston that Neville had wanted to develop Hedon Aerodrome but was opposed in doing so. Neville himself expressed to the Corporation that he had received a lot of support from various aero clubs and 'people of influence', but Mr Alston and the Corporation felt they were 'out on a limb'. In their view, it was wrong for an individual such as Neville to carry the torch. The article went on to quote Councillor L. Johnson, who suggested that it seemed wrong that some countries had spacecraft, yet Hull did not have a basic helipad. The Chairman of the Town Planning Committee was quoted as saying that whilst the Corporation would have supported an application to use Hedon as a flying club, another site had to be found.

On the 31 May, Mr Coulson M.P. invited Neville to London, to personally discuss the airfield matter. Upon reading the news on the Corporation's search, Neville found it to be very encouraging and wished the Corporation every success. He suggested however, that unless the Ministry were not pressed, then they might fail to react. He also felt that the Corporation had been badly let down by the Ministry and he consequently offered his help to them regarding aviation matters, should they require it.

Resuming contact with Mr Coulson M.P., Neville revealed in a letter dated 14 June that he had set up an interview with the Ministry of Aviation in London for the 1 June. Despite intending to attend with the Chairman of the Association of British Aero Clubs and Centres, he unfortunately became seriously ill two days prior to the interview and Neville had to proceed solo. He felt the interview was a disappointment, and he was unimpressed with their stance on the matter. In his view, they were unwilling to accept any argument for an aero club there.

As the Hull Corporation were pursuing the Ministry, it seemed the question of whether Hedon was ruled out had yet to be answered. Neville himself believed that the use of Hedon as the municipal airport of Hull was still a valid one and he offered to speak with Mr Coulson regarding this. Indeed a day later, Mr Alston acknowledged Neville's offer of help and stated that he would write to him again should he need it.

On the 22 June, Neville wrote to Mr Alderman F. Holmes, O.B.E, the then Chairman of the Development Committee at the Hull Corporation. He had expressed concerns that the Corporation had 'lost heart' in the Hedon project and that something must be done to combat this. Mr Holmes responded by saying that whilst he admired his efforts, the Corporation had 'gone to the limit in pressing the case for Hedon' and was at a loss to see how he could help at this stage. Mr Holmes also stated that the Council had already shown interest in the establishment of an airport to the east of Hull. Later in July, Mr Coulson M.P. responded to Neville's letter and confirmed that he would meet him the week commencing the 25 September.

Following a holiday abroad which included a stay at Rotterdam, Neville updated Mr Alston on his thoughts towards the Hedon project. During his stay, he visited the city's port and nearby airport situated north of it. He commented on how both the airport and heliport appeared to be very active, remarking on what a boon it would be for Hull to have an air link with Rotterdam. He suggested that Hull's importance would inevitably increase if Britain entered the European Common Market and that the need for air links to the continent from Hull would become imperative should this take place.

Throughout the months prior, Neville had made approaches to three different landowners in Hutton Cranswick in the quest for an airfield. One landowner, who was initially interested, changed his mind after an apparent 'go-ahead', which Neville saw as a great pity. His plot was almost ideal despite its distance from the city. Consequently, he was back again to looking for an alternative site in the East Riding, but his trouble had been finding a landowner sufficiently interested in flying to rent off a portion of land for this purpose.

The death of the Chairman of the Association of British Aero Clubs and Centres back in June jeopardised the flying club's case with the Ministry of Aviation. Neville imagined that he would face great difficulty in finding anybody as passionate and determined as him but, despite this tragic setback, he hoped to put forward a good case when he intended to meet with Mr Coulson M.P. during the week of the 25 September.

As the Ministry of Aviation were still, by 1961, willing to license Hedon Aerodrome to their standards, Neville again put forward a planning application to the Holderness Rural District Council to use the site for flying purposes. In support of this, he enclosed a small ordnance survey map with the proposed and amended runway layout. The main east and west runway would be one thousand yards long with an alternative subsidiary runway running NW to SE at about 575 yards long. These changes took into consideration all of the hazards at that point, including the railway, the roads and the unusable ground near the Distillers Company factories.

Neville could find no valid reason why the whole of the land could not be used, as from an official planning point of view he believed there was little fault in the amended layout, which he hoped would settle the argument. Over one thousand yards separated the factory from the proposed runway and even if further developments occurred, there would still be five hundred yards between any buildings. The layout, he argued, ensured safety for the club and allowed aircraft to operate with ease. A small amount of surface work would be required, but this was comparatively a non-issue.

The meeting with Mr Coulson M.P. took place as planned on the 28 September, with the topic of discussion being the potential possibilities and ways to get on with the Hedon Aerodrome. The meeting began with the theory that if the Hull Corporation were to push hard for planning permission to use Hedon, they might well succeed. Alternatively, if Neville's club reapplied for planning permission, this would mean a further appeal which they would need to pay for, and there was an extreme likelihood that it would fail again. As the Distillers Company and others would likely request a reimbursement for these costs, this was a prospect that the club could not face. Mr Coulson seemed keen on doing something in respect of the airfield and was quite prepared to start pushing the Hull Corporation into taking action. At that time, the matter was constantly being deferred.

An article published in the Hull Daily Mail, entitled 'May be Hull Airport', revealed that the Hull Corporation had approached British aircraft manufacturer Blackburn Aircraft Limited to discuss the possibilities of the Brough airfield being used for civil air traffic. At the time, the aircraft company had a factory on the site. The Corporation were to approach other companies with the aim of gathering interest in a local airport, and this would eventually supplement market research they were looking to conduct on the subject. The decision to pursue Brough had been authorised by the Town Planning Committee, after a preliminary investigation into a proposed airport was submitted. The report argued that an ideal airport should be as near as possible to the city and whilst Hedon airfield was mentioned, it was promptly disregarded.

After reading the news, Neville doubted whether Blackburn Aircraft would agree to anything like this, considering the company had recently been taken over by the Hawker Siddeley Group. They might also reject, he added, on the basis of security as their NA 39 Buccaneer aeroplane was still under production and test flying had been taking place. This testing was taking place not at Brough, but at Holme-on-Spalding-Moor instead. Still adamant that Hedon was more than suitable for the purposes of a local airfield, he argued that the runway at Brough was shorter than the one at Hedon, in any event.

On the occasions that Neville and the flying club had approached Blackburn Aircraft, they had opposed frequent use of their aircraft by 'outsiders'. The company however had been extremely helpful in other ways and prior to the planning issues arising, had planned on subsidising the club so that their employees could obtain flying licences at Hedon. The comparison between Brough and Hedon was, in his view, rather ironic. Blackburn Aircraft, a large employer of around 4,000 staff, lay directly at one end of the runway at Brough although he felt that nobody seemed to mind this. Comparatively, at Hedon, the Distillers Company were also large employers but more remote with considerably fewer personnel involved. Despite this, they had still kicked up a fuss regarding any flying taking place.

At the same time, proposals had been drafted on the basis of erecting a completely new airport development within the city of Hull, with possible sites mentioned including Newport, situated west of the city, Swine, north east of the city and Brough, which already had an established airfield. Both Swine and Newport had the advantage of being able to accommodate two full length runways, although Brough, which was already established, was much more conveniently situated in relation to the city itself. Adapting Brough would have obviously been cheaper, but an extension to the airfield itself would have proved extremely difficult due to its location. Brough was also home to a military aircraft manufacturer, and this meant that any civil operator would be required to share space with them. This would potentially lead to difficulties in congestion, as well as security.

The costs of implementing such a development were estimated, which included three separate estimations for a full international airport, an intermediate scheme with the possibility of an extension, and a small airport for use by charter services and a flying club, with no additional land required for future extension. These were itemised as seen below:

Cost of Developing a Full International Airport (1961):

Land	£250,000
Runways (2 x 10,000 feet)	£1,300,000
Terminal building	£1,000,000
Other facilities	£1,000,000
Total	£3,550,000

Cost of Intermediate Scheme with Possibility of Extension (Minimum) 1961:

Land	£250,000
Runways (2 x 5,000 feet)	£650,000
Temporary terminal building	£100,000
Other facilities	£300,000
Total	£1,300,000

Cost of Small Airport for Charter Services and a Flying Club with No Land Acquired for Extension (1961):

Land	£20,000
Runways (1 x 2,500 feet)	£162,000
Terminal building	£250,000
Other facilities	£250,000
Total	£682,000

Other costs would include a perimeter track, apron, lighting hangars and roads.

On the 3 November, Mr Hullock of the Ministry of Transport and Civil Aviation contacted Neville, stating that he had never changed his official attitude or recommendation, upheld by the Ministry, to allow for an aerodrome licence to be issued at the Hedon Aerodrome. This was providing planning permission was sought and approved first. As the flying club had recently altered the proposed runway design at the airfield, he warned that after allowing for the safe clearances of roads, railway, houses and other developed areas, the site would only just be large enough to operate the smallest aircraft, although this would be adequate for a small flying club such as the East Yorkshire Aero Company.

At that time, the trend in executive flying was for larger aircraft. Whilst private flying was exempt from legislation governing the safety margins of take-off and landing, Mr Hullock argued that for an aerodrome to be of any value, it should be able to accept any type of aircraft including larger ones. He also went on to say that even if the aerodrome was opened in a small way at first, it could prove to be a 'white elephant' for a local authority if it did not allow for expansion and development. Hedon did not possess any development potential beyond a basic flying club. He added that whilst a club could operate successfully within these limitations, it would be difficult to recommend such an aerodrome to the Hull Corporation as, before long, they would need to search for a larger site. With the outcome of the appeal, there would be little use in 'whipping a dead horse', he suggested.

On the 7 November, Mr Hullock dispatched a letter to Mr Coulson M.P. about his experiences with the Hull Corporation. He had found cooperation with the Corporation 'impossible' and whilst several officials and councillors were helpful, the official attitude there appeared 'completely negative'. Their manner seemed to rule out Hedon, and from Mr Coulson's point of view, he had been dissatisfied about the information given on the types of aircraft that could be used at the airfield. The Corporation had also apparently refused to investigate proposals to use Brough Aerodrome, despite being seen in the wider community as Hedon's successor.

Two weeks later, Neville informed Mr Hullock that he intended to reapply for planning permission to use Hedon Aerodrome for the following flying purposes:

1. A Flying Club.
2. A Business and Executive Aircraft Terminal
3. Charter Passenger/Freight Services with STOL Aircraft (mainly Twin-Pioneers of British United Airways).

These uses would be with appropriate aircraft under daylight flying rules. The reason he wished to reapply, he revealed, was due to the Corporation's renewed interest in opening an airport within the city. He argued that, with the impending closure of the Withernsea to Hull Railway Line, a fair amount of land north of the present line would be made available and could be used by a flying club.

In response, Mr Hullock highlighted that the Ministry's original position on licensing Hedon Aerodrome, providing it was based on the original requirements, was still in effect. He went on to add that whilst it would not be necessary for private aircraft to use licensed aerodromes, it would not be good practice to invite operators to use an aerodrome which only offered the minimum distance and smallest of safety margins in case of misjudgement by the pilot. Not all pilots are 'exceptional' he added and the Ministry's recommended safety landing and take-off distances requirements should be ideally put in place.

Mr Hullock felt that Hedon was much too limited for public transport operations and he seriously wondered if Neville had considered the full implications of this, considering the few aircraft that could actually operate there. The issues surrounding wind also arose and whilst there would be little issue if the wind direction was easterly or westerly, the problem of an alternative landing site in other wind directions could deter operators. If the club were to advertise the aerodrome for general charter use then the Ministry, he added, may not be so willing in granting a licence, if it could not calculate a usability factor of around 95%.

In a letter published in the Hull Daily Mail entitled 'Municipal Airports Do Not Pay', the writer, a Mr Boydell of Westella, congratulated the Hull City Council on their 'sensible' rejection of the suggestion that they could provide the city with an airport. He argued that the costs of doing so would be 'so much for so little' and suggested that the towns that do have them are constantly swallowing their pride and importuning the Government for financial assistance.

The aero club pressed ahead and resubmitted their planning application on the 8 December. The application was accepted on the 13 December, with a decision expected to be made by the 12 February 1962. In the application, the proposed development was outlined as for the following:

1. Landing ground for business and executive aircraft.
2. Landing ground for suitable light charter aircraft.
3. A flying club base.

A covering letter was enclosed with the application, explaining some of these points. Neville stressed that the use of the old airfield would be limited to aircraft of appropriate operational limits, as laid down by the aircraft flight manuals. He reiterated that the Ministry of Aviation maintained strict control of aviation matters and that they were still prepared to issue an aerodrome licence for the Hedon site, limited to certain types of aircraft deemed appropriate for the size of the site. If subsequent developments were to take place, the Ministry would not issue a licence should their regulations be infringed. This was a last-ditch attempt by the club to carry on flying at Hedon.

In response to Mr Boydell's letter, Neville felt that it was 'imperative for Hull to have (an) airfield'. After he had attended a meeting at The Guildhall in November where some councillors had rejected the recommendation to investigate the possibility of a Hull airport, he stressed that this was an inquiry without any obligation on the council and overall, this was a backwards step. Listening to comments by some senior councillors, in his view, they possessed an attitude toward flying more appropriate for the thirties than the sixties.

In response to the £3 million figure quoted by Mr Boydell, Neville argued that this was misleading as the figure was to construct a fully international airport on untouched land. In this instance, such an elaborate layout would not be required and a quarter of this amount would be sufficient to build a smaller airport catering for Hull's needs. He claimed that Hull could not afford to be without an airport and the longer it did the Humber estuary may became something of a depressed area, unable to compete with the more progressive ports.

On the 12 December, the East Yorkshire Aero Company reapplied to the East Riding County Council for planning permission, for use of Hedon for flying purposes. Neville had been extremely disappointed with the council's attitude on the issue of a Hull airport, especially after the hard work put into the project. Additionally, the Hull Junior Chamber of Commerce were now receiving replies to a questionnaire on whether the city's industry required air services and this would be revealed later on.

DEATH OF AN AIRPORT:

The Hedon Aerodrome Saga

1962

Kicking off the New Year, the flying club began to make preparations for holding a demonstration at Hedon, intended to drum up support. Further on from their planning application a month prior, Neville felt that one of the reasons for the refusal of permission was that they were unable to put forward their case in the best possible way. A good way of doing this, he felt, would be to demonstrate the aircraft intended for use on the airfield. The club were now in a position to do this and he aimed at gathering some aircraft together within the next couple of months.

The flying club aimed to have at least a dozen or so aircraft available for the occasion, hoping to attract as many interested people as possible. The event, Neville argued, would allow heads of industry, councillors and other great and good of the area to experience modern aircraft and to see the airfield in action. There was also the possibility of a flight over Hull, if anybody wished. A demonstration such as this he believed would not only help the cause but impress those present. The club had already received confirmation from Sir Robert McAlpine, the civil engineering firm, offering to bring along the company's Helio Super Courier. Mr Kenneth McAlpine, Director of the company and a pilot himself, had earlier been featured in an article entitled 'Hedon Airfield Hazard is a Myth – Pilot' about comments he had made at a conference, attended with the engineering company Priestman Bros.

During the conference, he revealed that it was the first time he had heard of an 'industrial undertaking objecting to a mythical hazard'. When asked if there were any hazards to the surrounding villages or buildings, he replied, 'none at all, the only hazards are to premises in direct line with the runways, or when an engine fails on take-off or an aircraft overshoots a landing'. Sir Robert McAlpine had an aviation division based at Luton Airport with Mr McAlpine, and the Director had reportedly approached the Board of Directors at the Distillers Company in an effort to influence them regarding Hedon.

The aero club were also in contact with the Business Aircraft Users Association (BAUA) who had offered to assist in arranging other aircraft to be present at a demonstration. One of their sources was said to be Newcastle Airport. All in all, Neville felt that this was a golden opportunity to help the aviation cause in the city of Hull. He also hoped that representatives of the council could be present when the demonstration was taking place, especially those involved with the decision on the planning matter. He was quite sure that those who attended would be 'favourably impressed'.

Once again however, the club were refused planning permission to fly from Hedon. Despite this, Neville persevered and the flying club arranged a demonstration at the airfield from the 6-8 of March. The bulk of the aircraft to be in attendance would be supplied through the BAUA, with around fifteen to twenty aircraft of various types including Cessnas, Pipers, Piaggios and Austers expected to attend. Neville would also receive assistance from the Hull Junior Chamber of Commerce, who would ensure that heads of industry be present at the event.

The Ministry of Aviation were also invited to attend but the club wanted to confirm beforehand whether private aircraft could operate from an unlicensed airfield. By private operation, they referred to an owner's aircraft carrying a firm's employees or goods as it was hoped the demonstration could go ahead without any legal ramifications. Mr Hullock, having not visited the site for some time, warned Neville that unless a lot of work had been done to smooth the runway at Hedon, a light aircraft could be seriously damaged during take-off.

The Town Planning Committee raised no objections to the club's proposal of holding a flying demonstration and it seemed that all was going to plan. All that was needed now was permission from the occupant of the land, the farmer Mr Smith. Scottish Aviation, the Scottish aircraft manufacturer, were also invited to attend and by this time, the date for the demonstration was set for the 8 March.

The flying club withdrew the training aspect from their planning application, only allowing qualified pilots to use the airfield. As this appeared to be at the heart of The Distillers Company concerns, Neville was willing to come to a compromise on the matter. Most importantly, any flying was better than none at all. The club requested that when the current tenancy ran out, that they be considered for use of the land should The Distillers Company withdraw their objection.

March brought the inevitable press coverage of the planned flying demonstration, with the Hull Daily Mail publishing an article entitled 'New Bid to Bring Back Airport – Flying Demonstration Planned for Hedon' describing the upcoming event. The article revealed how the men who 'fought most strongly' against the return of planes, referring to the East Riding planning people and Saltend industrialists, had been invited to attend. It was said that around twenty light planes would land, take-off and fly circuits in the hope of raising local interest in the airfield, aiming to show that planes could operate from the field without danger to the neighbouring industries and homes.

NEW BID TO BRING BACK AIRPORT

FLYING DEMONSTRATION PLANNED FOR HEDON

A FLYING DEMONSTRATION on the former Hedon aerodrome, which has been twice banned for flying in the past three years, is being planned for next month. And the men who have fought most strongly against the return of planes to Hull's prewar airport—the East Riding planners and Saltend industrialists—will be among those invited to watch.

The demonstration, at which about 20 light planes will land, take-off and fly circuits, is being planned by East Yorkshire Aero Company, Ltd.

Objects of the exercise are to raise interest locally in the reopening of Hedon for flying, and to show that planes can operate from the field without creating danger to neighbouring industries and homes.

In September, 1959, the East Riding County Council refused to allow the organisation to use 60 acres of the drome as a private airfield on the grounds that nearby industry would be threatened.

APPEAL FAILED

An appeal against the ban was turned down by the Minister of Housing and Local Government after a public inquiry had heard opposition from the Distillers Co. Ltd., which has millions of gallons of highly inflammable substances on a 100-acre Saltend site, and from the British Transport Commission, which was anxious about the petroleum plant there.

Within the past month another application by East Yorkshire Aero Co. Ltd., has been refused by Holderness Rural Council on the same grounds as before. Hedon Borough Council has renewed its previous opposition.

Mr Neville Medforth, a Hull businessman-pilot, who is one of the aero company's founders, told the Hull Daily Mail he hoped that the county planners would have deferred consideration of the latest application until they had had an opportunity of seeing the demonstration.

QUESTION OF SUPPORT

Whether or not the company appealed against the new refusal would depend very much on the support forthcoming after next month's demonstration.

Mr J. Williamson, East Riding County Planning Officer, said the application, with a recommendation from him, went to Holderness RDC, who had power to refuse it.

Despite the two planning refusals on use of the drome for flying, the demonstration could probably go on without breaking planning law, said Mr Williamson. The planning acts said that a person could use land for any purpose for up to 28 days.

mission to be there and we do not want to allow something which is going to put those industries out of business.

"We have been invited to the demonstration, but I do not think anyone will go."

PROPERTY RIGHTS

Mr Medforth told the Hull Daily Mail, "So far as I am concerned I think we could carry on flying all year round. If you got a group a people with private aircraft who would fly from Hedon, and the Corporation, as owners, would give permission, I don't think the East Riding County Council could stop us, provided we did not infringe the rights of private property in congested areas. To fly publicly, of course, you need the airfield licensed."

The one-day demonstration is being planned for March 8.

It has the backing of the Business Aircraft Users' Association, a national organisation supported by most of the country's biggest companies, which campaigns for the retention of suitable landing places for businessmen's planes.

Hull Corporation have given permission, subject to agreement by the farmer tenant of the land.

"WITHOUT DANGER"

Planes will be owned mostly by business users and may include Doves, Austers, Pipers, Cessnas and Piaggios.

Invitations to watch will probably go out to men from all the district's biggest industrial concerns, councillors and planners.

"I hope to get representatives from the Saltend industries—particularly from Distillers, who have been the main objectors to our proposals," said Mr Medforth.

"We believe that planes can operate from Hedon without danger to industry in the area. It was done before the war, and planes and navigation systems are much better now."

New Bid to Bring Back Airport – Flying Demonstration Planned for Hedon.
Hull Daily Mail (Mar. 1962)

A sales manager at Scottish Aviation revealed to Neville in a letter that he found it most surprising that a city as important as Hull was not served by even the most basic of airports and that attempts by his club in reopening Hedon had resulted in failure. The Scottish Aviation employee believed that the most basic of obstacles was the lack of air mindedness of the population and that too many people saw an aircraft as a 'collections of sticks and strings'.

Scottish Aviation were however extremely keen in supporting the aim of the reopening of Hedon and they felt the presence of a Twin Pioneer aircraft could prove to be in both parties' interests. Unfortunately, the company did not have a demonstration craft available at the time so, as such, could not attend. Nevertheless, they suggested that a Twin Pioneer would have no issue operating there and could certainly prove useful in its adaptability during operation (for example, being able to adapt from a 16-seater plane one day to freight the next). Whilst the company could not loan the use of a demonstration aircraft, they did recommend he contact Bristow Helicopters who happened to have one for sale.

A few days later the club received a disappointing setback, having been unable to secure consent from Mr Smith in using the land for a demonstration. This was disappointing, with the preparation work going to waste. The reasons, according to Mr Smith, were not financial (as cash was offered) but according to him there would be lambs and sheep on the airfield which he did not wish to be disturbed. By that Monday however, the airfield had been deserted and had been throughout the previous two months. Neville expressed his extreme annoyance at Mr Smith's attitude and felt that his refusal was a deliberate excuse in preventing the demonstration from being held, especially as his decision had only come about a week prior to it taking place.

The question now was where would the club go from here? The feelings of some industrialists in the city were that every effort should still be made to hold the demonstration as soon as possible and this was in line with Neville's own thoughts. With this setback, much depended on his next approach to The Distillers Company and annoyingly enough, a small plot of land in the corner of the airfield was being used as an argument against the point of flying at Hedon.

LAMBS BEFORE AIR DISPLA

A SUTTON farmer has explained why he could not allow the use of the former Hedon airfield for a display today by 20 light aircraft.

A Hull businessman-pilot, Mr Neville Medforth, planned the demonstration to show that the Hedon site could safely be used for flying.

As already reported in the Hull Daily Mail, Mr Medforth had to call off the display because the airfield was not available.

Mr Stamford Smith, a Sutton farmer who rents the field from Hull Corporation, said today, "I am far from wanting to stop the show, but I must consider my own business."

THROUGH SUMMER

Mr Medforth, he said, approached him about a month ago. He agreed to allow the field to be used for the display at a suitable time, but did not know how he would be situated in the near future.

He now had about 100 ewes and new-born lambs on the field.

"I could not allow planes to land among that lot. Lambs run towards anything approaching, rather than away from it."

Lambs were still arriving and would be feeding off the field throughout the summer.

He told Mr Medforth, who went to stake out the field two or three days ago, that the show could not take place at present, but that if he made an approach in the late summer, it would be considered.

March 1962 – Lambs Before Air Display, Hull Daily Mail

In March 1962, the Hull Daily Mail published an article entitled 'Lambs before Air Display' revealing how the Sutton farmer Mr Smith had agreed use of the site but later changed his mind as he 'could not allow planes to land among that lot'. He was referring to about a hundred ewes and lambs that had just been born on the field. He stated that 'lambs run towards anything approaching, rather than away from it'.

At this time, Neville was in discussions with a number of farmers who were prepared to graze the Hedon site. The BAUA suggested that if the Hull Corporation, backed by local industries, pressed hard enough then they could obtain usage for flying despite the neighbouring Distillers Company objection. Having made a visit to the company, Neville believed that they might agree to a limited usage by qualified pilots which, in any event, would be better than no flying whatsoever.

In the meantime, another site had been considered suitable for trainee pilots, an ex-RAF wartime bomber station at Pocklington with 'bags of room'. It was suitable, Neville suggested, for carrying a maintenance set-up and the possible operation of fairly large craft, as well as a flying club. The only apparent drawback was that it was twenty-five miles or so from Hull, but he suggested that it could be used in conjunction with Hedon. For example, he envisaged aircraft being kept and maintained at Pocklington and then flown to Hedon. In poorer weather, Pocklington would make a suitable alternative. If all else failed, he hoped that by taking on the grazing rights at Hedon himself, demonstrations could take place throughout the year unhindered.

The former RAF station at Pocklington

[Courtesy of Paul Francis]

It was still hoped that a demonstration would go ahead and the date now given for it was the 15 March. Despite Neville visiting The Distillers Company personally in the hope of persuading them to allow use of the airfield, negotiations had failed. One thing that he wanted to make clear however, was that had he considered flying from Hedon unsafe he would have abandoned the project straight away. A large chunk of the airfield in the southwest corner had also been chopped out as a gesture of goodwill, which according to the Ministry, they did not need to do. The offer to withdraw club training was a further reaction to conjecture on why the company were against their plans. In any event, the search for alternative club training accommodation proved to be a difficult and inconvenient task and Neville believed that their objection had effectively halted the development of air facilities within the Hull area.

The flying club received little consolation when a conversation with a company employee proved disappointing. Whilst the General Manager of The Distillers Company, Mr Allen, could apparently not recall discussions relating to the airfield taking place, he did provide the club with copies of maps and plans from three years prior. Neville suggested that this was probably because the matter was just a routine affair to him, as somebody who he imagined would be dealing with lots of different things on a daily basis.

Neville still believed that the objection in 1959 by The Distillers Company was odd, especially as he was under the impression that the company already knew about the club's plans in 1958 from press coverage. He felt that had the objection come through then, large sums of money spent on legal fees, an appeal and applications would have been saved. Mr Allen agreed to bring up the matter at the next London board meeting.

In a letter written two days later, Scottish Aviation commented on the suggested usage of the former RAF station at Pocklington as a secondary aerodrome for the Hull area. The writer agreed that it would be much too far from Hull to be a successful service and for one to be introduced to a 'non-air minded public', it must cause no inconvenience whatsoever. Travelling twenty-five miles for this would be unacceptable, he added.

The Distillers Company reiterated their position that they would oppose any future application for the use of the site for flying purposes, due to the potential dangers surrounding it. This was obviously disappointing to the club and to Neville, who had hoped he could perhaps convince the company to allow flying. On the 11 April, Mr Alston confirmed that the Hull Corporation had decided to re-let the Hedon site on a grazing term to the existing tenant and consequently, for another year at least, the site was off-limits for flying. This decision proved rather disappointing for the flying club, whose cause was featured in a leaflet produced by the Labour Party in rather cynical terms.

On the 18 May, an *Air Services Survey* produced by the Junior Chamber of Commerce concerning local air facilities for the Hull area was released. The report, signed by a Mr J. Ryan, found that 'were air facilities available, the businessmen of this city (Hull) would take advantage of them. They would also be a means of attracting new industries to the city.' 233 replies were received from all manner of businesses within the city and its surrounding areas. Forty-one stated that their businesses did not need to travel to London but, in twelve of those cases, could appreciate that such a service would benefit the overall business community. At the time, an average of 976 business trips were being made to London from Hull each month: 124 of these were by private car and 852 by rail. The report highlighted that there was definitely a need for speedy and efficient Hull to London transport links.

The report concluded that air services would be in the best interests of Hull-based ports and would complement the vast redevelopment of the dock facilities being carried out at the time. The potential advantages to international shipping were considered numerous and reiterated the notion of Hull being the only major port in the UK which did not have an airfield. An airport would have also ensured, the writer argued, that East Yorkshire would not become a future forgotten area. Research into the potential costs of implementing such a facility proved unsuccessful, but it was assumed that tremendous pressure would have to be brought to bear on the various powers that be to make it happen.

DO YOU KNOW?

The Conservatives on the Hull City Council
proposed spending

£2,750,000

of your money on an Aerodrome for the use
of a few Business men. At the same time they
supported the Conservative Government in
putting up the price of Welfare Foods for
Children and Babies.

North Newington Tories were the chief movers
in these proposals!

**Millions for
the Wealthy**

**Sacrifices from
the Needy**

Vote Labour leaflet – 1962

The subsequent months would prove rather sluggish in terms of progress, but in mid-September two articles were published entitled 'Hedon Airfield for Business' and 'Hedon Airfield Hazard is a Myth – Pilot'. The first article highlighted how businessman Mr Kenneth McAlpine, then Director of Sir Robert McAlpine, had flown into Hull via Hedon for business consultations with the firm Priestman Bros. Shortly after 11 am his scarlet monoplane, an American-built Helio Courier, was sighted over the River Humber. The plane landed at the airfield from Mr McAlpine's home in Kent after around 1 hour and 20 minutes of travelling.

The Helio Courier plane at Hedon Aerodrome with Directors of the East Yorkshire Aero Company (21 September 1962)

Mr McAlpine went on to discuss the airfield and its neighbouring factories, expressing that 'Saltend (was) no problem at all – you completely avoid it'. The Director was a former RAF pilot during the Second World War, becoming a flying instructor later on. In the later article, Mr McAlpine went on to say 'it (was) the first time I have heard of an industrial undertaking objecting to a mythical hazard'. Asked if there was hazard to the surrounding villages, he replied 'none at all, the only hazards are the premises in line with the runways when an engine fails on take-off or an aircraft overshoots on landing'.

Another article published later on entitled 'Goodbye to Hedon Airfield' revealed how the then Chairman of the Hull Town Planning Committee, Alderman Body, stated 'I think we can say goodbye to Hedon Aerodrome as an aerodrome'. He had been replying to an amendment which proposed that The Distillers Company, who leased part of the airfield as playing fields, would only be allowed to put a pavilion there for three years. Alderman Jackson stated that it would be a mistake to grant permanent planning permission on the site, which could still be used as an aerodrome. The Chairman reminded members that the Ministry of Transport had ruled out the notion that the aerodrome could not be reopened.

Despite the committee's sentiments, the October 1962 edition of the *Port of Hull Journal*, produced by Hull and Humber Ports, argued that it would 'be comforting' to have an airport that can handle the big airliners: 'What Hull does need now is a smaller, but fully and properly equipped airport that can handle the ever increasing volume of short and medium distance air traffic. The kind of traffic, actual and potential, that has led to the outlay of vast sums of money by the aircraft industry in producing a whole new generation of smaller airlines, vital in the pattern of modern air transport. Time is important because air routes are developing along certain paths. Once established, they are unlikely to change and the areas off the beaten track may become the back wood of the air age.'

Whilst the Hedon Aerodrome dream appeared to be dissolving for the East Yorkshire Aero Company, there still appeared to be great support for the reopening of the airfield. Indeed, in a letter sent to the Town Clerk on the 8 November, Neville argued that there were still interested people quite willing to take on the financial burdens of equipping, maintaining and running the airfield as a functional airport. He argued that the site at Hedon could safely be put to a number of uses in connection with flying (private, business and commercial) and suggested two airline companies that would be interested in supplying a regular passenger service from Hedon to London.

DEATH OF AN AIRPORT:

The Hedon Aerodrome Saga

1963

Despite a disappointing year previously in terms of aviation development, an article featured in the Hull Daily Mail on the 7 January entitled 'Hull to look again at air prospects' renewed hopes of a potential aviation industry within Hull. Indeed, the article revealed that despite the Hull Corporation ruling out a national airport near Hull two years previously, new advice had been sought and talks had been 'ordered' between the Corporation's Planning and Development Committees on the matter.

This time however, the Corporation were looking at all of the possibilities available, from services by helicopter to winged aircraft and from a small terminal near Hull to a major international airport. A planning sub-committee report highlighted two points over the future of the Hedon airfield. The committee voted to tell a private inquirer that the now disused airport could not be used for a flying club, in view of the Ministry of Housing and Local Government's ruling. The committee also considered a letter from Priestman Bros. Ltd, enquiring whether the airfield would be available for future landings of small aircraft. Several months prior, a private plane with a very important visitor had been allowed to land there and the firm was told that applications for landings would be considered on a merit basis.

In response to a letter dated 8 November 1962, Mr Haydon, the Town Clerk at the Hull Corporation, responded by saying that in view of the decision by the Ministry of Housing and Local Government on appeal, relating to the proposed use of the Hedon Aerodrome site, permission would not be granted on using it for flying. The consideration of civil airport facilities to serve the city of Hull, however, was still ongoing.

Interest was still being expressed in using the site, when on the 10 March a member of the public wrote to the club revealing how he had anxiously awaited a time when he could take flying lessons and enrol. Consequently, Neville expressed disappointment in the apparent 'wait and see' attitude that had been adopted by the council, following a meeting in relation to local air facilities. Embarrassingly his East Yorkshire Aero Club was now the only flying club in the United Kingdom without an aerodrome to its name.

Breaking his 'year long silence' on the issue, Neville, frustrated at 'banging his head against a wall for so long' and disappointed over the failure of his proposed flying demonstration at Hedon, felt that a 'bias' had been built up against him over his efforts to reopen Hedon. He therefore considered it a good idea to take a back seat for a while and see if anybody else could do better. He was pleased to read Mr McAlpine's comments on the usability of Hedon for business aircraft, as it confirmed in his mind that it was not just the 'idle comment of a layman' but the practical opinion of a very experienced pilot. This endorsed previous favourable comments regarding the airfield by test pilots at Blackburn Aircraft.

After hearing of delays regarding the newly formed sub-committee, he was not prepared to take any further setbacks 'lying down' after what now was the seventh year of striving for a local Hull air terminal. As it had been nearly twenty years since the end of World War II, and with the local council having failed to provide any air facilities since that time, it seemed to be the case in his mind that they were not interested in restarting flying from the city.

He argued that this would not matter so much were the council not the owners of the only existing airfield site near the city which, in any event, he felt they had allowed to steadily go to waste since 1939. It was significant in his mind that the Corporation were not prepared to venture into the realms of aviation despite effectively owning an airfield. Consequently, he had grown a resentment against the Corporation, based on the several years of 'fruitless effort' resulting in considerable losses in time and money.

He suggested that the Corporation as a local authority were empowered to re-purpose land for the use of flying, and yet had failed to press hard enough in obtaining use of the airfield which they already owned, or in finding other suitable land. The Corporation must have the power to 'beat down' a 'ridiculous' objection, especially when the Ministry appeared to be on the Corporation's side and were still apparently prepared to license Hedon as an airfield for flying, he suggested.

The flying club now had to store its aircraft at Yeadon, over seventy miles from Hull, and Neville felt that this arrangement was ridiculous. He was no longer prepared to stand back and take any further delays 'lying down' and had hoped to implement some flying locally before he became 'an old man'. To do this, he again requested the grazing rights for the land but was unsuccessful in securing them.

On the 28 March, Mr Alston confirmed that the Corporation had made the decision to contribute towards a survey, intended to discover the requirements for all kinds of facilities in Yorkshire and the North East. If the survey went ahead, then the results would be used to govern the Corporation's future actions with regard to air related matters.

In an article entitled 'Hull needs its own airport – councillor' published in the Hull Daily Mail on the 5 April, Councillor Sanderson was quoted as saying that a Yorkshire-based international airport would not fully solve Hull's air needs. He was commenting on a decision made by the council to send representatives to a meeting of the Yorkshire Airport Development Association, being held in York on the 25 March. He had hoped urgent progress would be made and that the matter was not something to keep 'in the pending tray'.

As the Leeds-Bradford airport in Yeadon was steadily developing, it seemed unlikely that a second major airport would be built in Yorkshire. That being said, Neville did not consider a local and an international airport to be the same thing and felt that the Corporation was tying itself too much to the idea of an airport to serve the whole of Yorkshire. A municipal airport for Hull would be far more important he argued and estimated that the present facilities at Hedon could be converted into a useful municipal airport for less than £5,000.

Despite this, Alderman Body, Chairman of the Town Planning Committee, suggested that there was no evidence of a demand for a Hull airport, but there was however evidence of the need for facilities to allow executive aircraft to land in the city. He suggested that as Hedon had been used for this purpose in the past, the Corporation could give permission for its use for a limited period in the future.

Another article was featured in the Hull Daily Mail over a month later entitled 'Hull-London Air Businessmen – Mr Priestman's plan', published on the 17 May. The article suggested that the summer period had looked to bring a new surge of interest in air transport within Hull and the East Riding, with a start expected on the Yorkshire Airport Development Association's investigations into the need for a large county international airport. It was suggested that such an airport be developed at Elvington.

Fresh talks were also being had on both small business and private flights from Hedon and Pocklington Aerodromes. It was certain that within the next few months, the Ministry of Housing and Local Government would order a public inquiry into a proposal by a Market Weighton businessman, Mr Robert Massey, to use the former RAF aerodrome at Pocklington for private flying. The Ministry said that as only two objections had been submitted against the proposals, it was probable the scheme would go through. In January, Mr Massey had bought 153 acres of the former airfield, including the control tower, for £19,950. A public inquiry concerning the old wartime bomber station was to be held on Tuesday the 12 November at Burnby Hall, Pocklington. In support of the project, Neville would attend alongside Mr Bray, a representative of the Association of British Aero Clubs and Centres.

Nearer to Hull, Mr James Priestman, the Director of Priestman Bros. Limited was considering new efforts to popularise Hedon Aerodrome for business flights. Mr Priestman had hoped to fly up to two dozen aircraft from a large international machinery exhibition in London to Hedon with their customers, for a tour of their factories which were close to the airfield. They had intended to travel back the same evening, as some of their customers were overseas visitors who were unable to spend more than two days travelling to and from the city. Mr Priestman, who had previously used Hedon for business operations, had hoped to wipe out the 'smear that Hedon is a comic airstrip and a danger to Saltend', so that other businessmen would use it with their own planes.

By October, new circulars were being distributed for the East Yorkshire Aero Company in the hope of building support for the club. Twelve members' slips were returned, with six as non-flying members and six as flyers. The letter assured potential members that despite Hedon being off-limits, another suitable aerodrome had been found after extensive searching.

On the 24 October, a twin-engine plane departed from the Hedon airfield carrying several businessmen, the largest to use the airfield since its closure before the war. The owners of the plane, Davy-Ashmore Group who were manufacturers of rolling mills and steel works, had no intention of using the field regularly with this an exception. It was simply that they were too late to take off from Leconfield, which they would have otherwise normally used.

Despite this, the company suggested that a strip such as Hedon would be extremely useful as it would allow them to fly on long summer evenings when Leconfield was closed. Captain John Formby, the pilot who made the landing on the bush-strewn grass, suggested that the field would be suitable for his plane but 'a bit tight for anything else'. The engineering company Priestman Bros. had also used the field and were interested in developing it, with the Director of the company Mr Priestman expressing his desire for an airfield close at hand. 'We are trying to show people that it can be used safely. There is no need for aircraft to fly over Saltend,' he stated. Industrialists who then used Leconfield faced a thirty minute journey to Hull. A twin-engine aircraft travelling to London would only take fifty minutes.

Landing at Hedon – a Beechcraft Queen Air registered G-ARFF of Davy-Ashmore Ltd. of Sheffield touches down on the Hedon Airfield, 23 October 1963 – Hull Daily Mail.

The East Yorkshire Aero Company, keen to retake on the grazing rights tenancy at Hedon, expressed a desire for these to be granted to them. On the 4 November, Mr Alston confirmed that this request made to the Town Planning Committee to tender for the grazing rights was not granted. Disappointed, Neville argued that if the Corporation were in favour of the revenues derived from the grazing of the airfield rather than the attempt to restart flying, then it would be virtually impossible for them to compete against a farmer who was also a cattle dealer.

This fact was obvious in his view as no revenue could be derived from the flying until planning permission was obtained, and the only revenue to offset the rental would be the grazing of a few local farmers. In conclusion, he suggested that if it were the policy of the Corporation to restart flying from Hedon, then planning permission must be applied for as soon as possible. In support of his request for grazing rights, the following reasons were put forward:

1. Request landings could be dealt with speedily and without fuss or trouble, which was not possible at the moment.
2. It is essential that the parts of the airfield which require to be levelled should be dealt with as soon as possible, as a stranger might find landing somewhat hazardous. Also, the fence towards the east end should be removed as this is preventing larger aircraft getting in and constitutes a hazard to all incoming aircraft. The levelling cannot be carried out unless the grazing rights are held by somebody prepared to do this. Two visiting aircraft had already been slightly damaged because of the above points.

On the 11 November, an article entitled 'Bid for Private Airfield' revealed how a special meeting was to take place with the Pocklington Town Council, who were considering a private airfield scheme at the former Pocklington Aerodrome. An inspector for the Ministry of Housing and Local Government was to be present to hear arguments for and against the plan. The plan had been put forward by the Market Weighton based motor dealer, Robert B. Massey and Co. Ltd., with Mr

Massey expressing a desire in opening the airfield for flying by private, business and executive aircraft. Three objectors had put forward concerns about the plan.

A day later, a follow-up article entitled 'Temptation Runways' was published in the Yorkshire Post. During the inquiry, it was found that the runways of the Pocklington Aerodrome were longer than needed for light aircraft and it was suggested that an operator would prefer to use it for larger aircraft. Several objectors stated that whilst they would not be against the use of small aircraft, they would be for larger craft. One of the objectors was a Mr A. Hessell, the owner of a section of industrial land near the airfield. In addition, a Mr Morris of York was investigating the possibility of starting a flying club in the York area, which would similarly offer teaching and a clubhouse to create interest in air touring and competitive flying.

DEATH OF AN AIRPORT:

The Hedon Aerodrome Saga

1964

By 1964, it was clear to the East Yorkshire Aero Club that the Hedon dream was long over. Neville had begun considering alternative sites to use as it was clear at this point that using Hedon was no longer a viable option. Demand for an airfield still appeared to be evident and an article published on the 12 February, entitled 'Pilot searches for Hull Airstrip', highlighted how the head of a Worcestershire based air-taxi firm, Tacair Limited, would start commercial services from Hull immediately if he could find a suitable airfield.

The Director of the company, Captain P. Beechey, was an ex-RAF and airline pilot who made the comments after the end of a second unsuccessful search for an airfield within the Hull area. He made reference to a survey he requested be carried out for him by the Hull Chamber of Commerce and Shipping, which stated that four out of five leading industrial firms in the Hull area would make use of air services from the city.

One company alone using rail links had requested a daily passenger service to London for up to eight people. Captain Beechey felt that there was definitely a requirement for air-taxi services from Hull, with London being the destination most in demand. Other places also requested included Manchester, Newcastle and Edinburgh. The Captain had asked the Hull Corporation for permission to fly from Hedon, however so far he had not received a response. He stated that 'if we fall down on Hedon, I think we shall have to pack the idea in for the time being'.

Neville wrote to the entire Town Planning Committee, spurred on by the release of the long-awaited report by the Yorkshire Airport Development Association, recalling how the Corporation's aerodrome policy would be decided after this was released. From briefly reading the survey, he concluded that it would be 'probably of no value to Hull' where air facilities were considered. He had completed a report of his own on the Hedon case and mentioned how a 1939 issue of the *Air Pilot* magazine, the final year of the aerodrome's operation, mentioned that The Distillers Company factory was something to be avoided. The airport still operated as normal, he argued. Indeed, the magazine states in its 1939 edition, that 'flight below an altitude of 1,000 feet above the Salt End Chemical Works should be avoided, owing to the inflammable nature of the material handled. The roof of these premises is marked with a white cross by day and by lights at night.'

On the 2 May, an article entitled 'Air taxi firm wants to fly from Hedon 'drome' revealed how Captain Beechey was to challenge the ban on reopening Hedon Aerodrome for flying, by putting forward his own planning application to use two hundred acres of the site as a licensed aerodrome. His application to the Holderness Rural District Council was for the: *provision of take-off, landing, hangarage, maintenance and all other facilities associated with the operation of aircraft and for the carriage of passengers and freight.* He was seeking permission to use an area of 4,000 feet by 1,980 feet.

Chairman of the Hull City Council Town Planning Committee Alderman Body, stated that the site 'had been written off' as a possible municipal landing strip for Hull because of the nearness of it to Saltend. Captain Beechey had hoped to operate charter flights in the first instance, but suggested that if he could make Hedon usable then he intended to establish scheduled services. He had written to the Hull Corporation asking for their permission to use the aerodrome and was told that the request would be considered by a joint planning and development sub-committee dealing with the whole issue of air facilities in Hull.

A letter written by Neville and published in the Hull Daily Mail with the title 'Pocklington-Hedon airport link' had suggested that the airfield at Brough would be unavailable for civil flying and could not be taken into account. The reason, he highlighted, was that for several years the manufacturer Hawker Siddeley had chosen to block its use on the grounds of security, despite requests from various operators. He mentioned how, famously, the entertainer Hughie Green had been barred from landing there three times in succession, eventually complaining. Eighteen months prior, Mr McAlpine was also apparently prevented from refuelling at Brough and had to do so at RAF Leconfield.

It seemed apparent that both Brough and Hedon Aerodromes had now been barred for public use. Despite the Second World War being won with air power, Neville argued that both local industry and authorities had failed to produce an operational air terminal in the nineteen years since the end of the war, suggesting that they were quite prepared to go on talking for an indefinite period. He had grown resentful of the slur that had been repeatedly cast on club flying and suggested that many famous pilots, both before and during the war, had taken part in the flying club movement. The Battle of Britain might not have been won were it not for those weekend flyers who later became our first line of defence, he proclaimed.

He felt that the Hull Corporation and the Chamber of Commerce had ignored a public inquiry which was held in November 1963, in connection with a proposed use of Pocklington Aerodrome as an airfield. This was approved and made possible by the foresight and financial commitments of Mr Massey, he stated, whose 'public-minded gesture must stand as a shining example in the face of the apathy of others'. Although asked to support the inquiry, the Hull Corporation and Chamber of Commerce failed to do so. As the aerodrome had a larger layout, he felt all support should be given to both Pocklington and Hedon Aerodromes as both, he argued, could satisfy the aviation needs of Hull and East Yorkshire at little expense to the authorities.

In a July article entitled 'Corporation split on air links?' Mr Claude Fisher, then President of the Hull Chamber of Commerce and Shipping, had remarked on how the Hull Corporation seemed 'split within itself' over the question of air links for the city. He added that 'it looked as if they have not yet formed their own views'. The Chamber had unsuccessfully tried to discuss the Yorkshire Airport Development Association report on air services in the northeast with the Corporation, which included information on the provision of take-off and landing facilities close to Hull. The Hull Advisory Committee of the Regional Board for Industry was also seeking to meet with the Corporation. Mr Fisher added that 'we are all agreed that we want an airfield or landing strip which can be used at any time and not, as now, with special permission having to be obtained every time'.

Meanwhile, the East Yorkshire Aero Company made a claim against the Hull Corporation for its losses on the Hedon project. In his letter, Neville stated that he was increasingly concerned over the continued lack of any flying facilities in the Hull area, as it had now been seven and half years since his first correspondence with them. He believed that had there been no planning involvement in the first instance, Hedon would most likely be a thriving little air terminal with four or five years operational experience behind it. Instead, he argued, a legacy of developing expenditure was created with no income whatsoever to offset it and with no apparent means of recovery.

It was for this reason that he made this request to the Corporation for the reimbursement of money laid out with the belief that flying could and would eventually commence at Hedon. He was saddened that he had to do this and obviously would have preferred to be operating from the site or an alternative. The Town Clerk of the Corporation responded by saying that there did not appear to be any liability on the part of the Corporation in contributing to the expenses which the club had incurred, as no prior agreement was set up for reimbursement. Despite this, it was agreed the matter would be forwarded on to the Town Planning Committee for consideration.

Neville argued that it was obvious from the start that substantial work and expenditure would be required in making the field at Hedon suitable for flying. Again, he felt that this agreement was clearly implied when they gave the go-ahead. In January 1957, he suggested that a figure of £3-5000 would be required in restoring the airfield for operation. By 1964, this figure had increased to £7,000. When the question of planning permission was originally raised by the Holderness Rural District Council, the Hull Corporation had apparently advised him to continue on the grounds that Hedon was the former Hull municipal airport and planning permission was not required.

With the threat of a ban by the East Riding County Council alongside The Distillers Company, he decided to hold all operations until the issue of planning had been resolved. In hindsight, he was glad he did, otherwise the expenses would have been even greater. Had the Corporation assured him at the time and covered any expenses that would have arisen as a result of the continuation of flying, he would have been happy to continue.

In 1957, at a time when nobody appeared remotely interested in tackling aviation in the Hull area, Neville had hoped to initiate some flying of sorts through club flying. Several years down the line, and with all the publicity surrounding his plight, he was resentful that local aviation had become a general topic of conversation. Still, charter and business aircraft had landed at Hedon despite all flying from the terminal being banned and he felt that were it not for his work in the late fifties, people would not be able to use the airfield at all.

He felt that a slur had been cast on club flying since his efforts and he regarded this as disgraceful. It was never his intention to stick solely to club flying, but began with this as he considered it the quickest way of raising interest in a local aero club. All in all, he believed that had it not been for the planning inquiry and the subsequent objections that arose from it, there would be no need for the compensation of his efforts. In fact, he felt that because nobody had suggested to him that planning permission should be sought, between 1957 and June 1959 the matter did not concern him. Indeed, the Town Planning Department of the Hull Corporation did not see fit for him to raise any planning concerns and it was assumed by all that as Hedon was once an established airfield, it would not be required.

He believed that the East Riding County Council had used its planning powers as an excuse to block aviation development in Hedon, satisfying the nearby works, namely The Distillers Company, to have no flying from the site. The company's objection always puzzled him, as it was apparent that they were aware of the airfield's activities as early as December 1958. Yet, for whatever reason, they did not object until September 1959. Although they apparently denied all knowledge of the airfield, he was never satisfied with this excuse and believed that the company's negotiations regarding the plot of land were taking place alongside his own club's negotiations.

He therefore outlined the aero club's expenditure up to that point, which was as follows:

Actual expenditure incurred, supported by vouchers, bank statements, etc. (available for inspection):   £620

Devaluation of aircraft over period: £250

Time spent by self and co-directors, including inconveniences over the past 5-6 years: £750

Other expenses (aircraft clearance, etc.) *estimated*   £80

Total: £1,700

The issue of compensation was considered by the Hull Corporation and it was decided on the 24 November that the club would receive no reimbursement towards any of its costs associated with the airfield at Hedon.

An article published on the 5 October entitled 'Hull airfield move' revealed how a meeting between two Hull Corporation committees recommended some provision be made for airfield facilities. During this, it was suggested that the Hull Chamber of Commerce collaborate with other organisations to agree on a definite plan moving forwards. Whilst Hedon would have been a good option, due to established risk to industrial operations Brough appeared to offer the readiest solution with an estimated cost of £570,000 in making it operational. There was also the possibility that the proposed private enterprise at Market Weighton could fully meet Hull's needs. One of the suggestions put forward by the committee was that information should be sought as to whether industrial firms, who would be the main users of the airfield, would be prepared to contribute to the cost of establishing it.

Flying to Hull via Hedon was Mr William Wallace, Director of Wallace & Jones Limited. The company was a Nottinghamshire based air-taxi firm that owned a Dornier Do 28A STOL plane (registration number G-ASUR). On the 21 October,

Mr Wallace had intended staging a demonstration at Hedon with the plane but, rather unfortunately, this had to be cancelled after it was damaged colliding with a pothole whilst taxiing on the airfield runway. Following the mishap, an engineer was dispatched from Leicester to inspect the aircraft and it was concluded that an engine mounting along with its undercarriage had been damaged. The plane could not be flown until it was repaired and estimations for this were put at £1,000. Fortunately, the repairs could be made under cover inside the former airfield hangar and the aircraft subsequently spent several days there whilst these were being carried out.

Dornier DO.28A-1 G-ASUR at Hedon Aerodrome (21 October 1964)

Courtesy of the Hull Daily Mail

DEATH OF AN AIRPORT:

The Hedon Aerodrome Saga

1965

With Hedon making the headlines, all manner of possible airfields began to be discussed in the desire for a local air service. On the 18 January, an article published in the Hull Daily Mail entitled 'Airfield: action is delayed' revealed how plans for a Pocklington airfield had been delayed until a 'nuisance' occurred. The decision had been confirmed by the Clerk of Pocklington Parish Council and later discussed in a letter to the newspaper by a Mr L. Sands. A recent commission on airfields had deemed a Pocklington Aerodrome unsuitable and in the letter, Mr Sands doubted if one would ever become an international airport. The proposed aerodrome would also potentially be restricted from night-time flying and Mr Sands stated that no action could be taken until a 'nuisance' had occurred. In any event the Parish Council supported the view that the matter be left for the time being.

It had now been eight years since Neville's flying club had first expressed interest in a Hull airport. With this, he submitted information to the Hull Corporation Town Planning Officer in view of the 'desperate need' for an airstrip near the city. Professing a bias toward Pocklington and Hedon, he felt that despite the former being rather remote (twenty-five miles from Hull City Centre) it had great potential as a scheduled service airport for both passenger and freight and could develop into a regional airport. This idea was under the assumption that Pocklington would operate as a main base alongside a satellite airstrip on the east side of Hull. With Hedon considered unavailable, he sought alternative sites for an airstrip and concluded that there were three possible choices:

1. <u>Bilton - Wyton</u> – five miles from Hull City Centre. Planning permission had already been applied for and the decision was expected within the next fortnight. Readily available, but at present was limited to around 700 yards. Suitable as a business aircraft terminal with up to 100 yards.
2. <u>Burton Constable</u> – nine miles from the Hull City Centre. Planning permission had been applied for but due to difficulties with the then current tenant, a decision may potentially be delayed for around 18 months. Possibly good potential for a feeder aerodrome.
3. <u>Oxgoddes</u> (South of Thorngumbald) – nine miles from Hull City Centre. Planning had not been applied for but no difficulties had been anticipated in getting it. The owner/occupier apparently would sell for around £40-50,000. Neville remarked that this was a good potential site, with plenty of room for development.

He still professed in having a preference toward the former Hedon airfield and even though it had been ruled as being out of the question many times, he reassessed Hedon being used as a satellite to Pocklington as 'first class'. He gave the following reasons:

- Hedon was only four miles from Hull's city centre and closer than the three aforementioned locations.
- Hedon had the greatest road access to the centre of Hull, via Hedon Road.
- Hedon could very effectively cater for the large docks and expanding industrial areas on the east side of Hull.
- The Hedon site was local authority owned.

- Its runway had a good surface requiring only superficial levelling in places.
- The airfield already had hangarage with water, electricity and telephone lines installed.
- The site was in close proximity to the Ottringham VOR beacon, which proved useful as a navigational aid in poor weather.
- The Ministry of Aviation were still prepared to issue an aerodrome licence for the site.
- Hedon had received recent use from business aircraft and had become well known in the business community. It was regarded as an established aerodrome and as a result (in his opinion) planning permission was not a requirement.

He cited a document circulated by the Ministry of Aviation to all the local authorities during 1963, which offered advice and guidance on the development of an unlicensed airfield. From a brief study of his notes, he suggested that the Ministry criteria for the creation of such an airstrip would be adequately fulfilled at Hedon. The idea behind such airstrips was to allow local authorities to provide facilities for the rapidly increasing business and executive flyers, with the unlicensed nature of the airstrips being considered more acceptable due to the low set-up costs involved.

For licensed airfields, Ministry of Aviation regulations did not permit charter aircraft exceeding 6,000 pounds (2,722 kg) in weight, with planning permission needing to be obtained before they would even issue a licence. These rules did not apply to unlicensed airstrips providing danger or nuisance is of no issue. With an outcry for flying facilities in the city, Neville believed that The Distillers Company would not dare oppose flying from Hedon now. He believed that the company's objection was sustained by one unnamed individual and this individual now found himself having to run with the hare and hunt with the hounds (i.e. agreeing with The Chamber of Commerce that flying facilities should be provided for Hull, whilst at the same time trying to prevent flying from

---

the most 'logical place', Hedon Aerodrome). It was this that he believed had prevented Hull from having proper air facilities for the previous five and a half years.

In his view, there was little reason why this state of affairs could not continue on a heavier scale with just a small number of changes. It had been possible for outside aeroplanes to fly into Hedon, but there were no provisions for local aircraft to fly out due to the lack of a suitable and modern hangar. He put forward three proposals to remedy this problem:

1. Terminating the present grazing arrangements would remove the hazard of grazing stock to aircraft. Mowing could be substituted for when the grass grew during the spring/summer.
2. Allow a company to level minor irregularities on the runway itself, including the removal of a fence running across the airfield north to south.

These two factors he argued had deterred fliers from using Hedon since his connections with the aerodrome began. He also suggested the following be implemented:

3. Allow home-based aircraft to access the existing hangarage, enabling 6 to 8 aircraft of the business and light charter type to be kept for outgoing use.

Whilst there would be the small loss of grazing revenue to the Hull Corporation, he suggested this would be countered by the hangar storage and landing fees, alongside potential revenues from the mowing (such as haymaking). With this, the Corporation could provide private air facilities at a low cost and resolve 'a headache' at the same time.

During a visit to the East Riding County Council planning department earlier in the week, Neville felt that they had adopted a 'rather smug attitude' upon discovering that the Hull Corporation were intending to approach the County Planning department. They were going to do this with a view to authorising air facilities, now there was no longer any suitable land within their city boundaries. He admitted to being rather unimpressed with their attitude.

Whilst the Hull Corporation were investigating the possibility of airfield facilities for the city, Town Planning Officer Mr Alston did not wish to comment on Neville's suggestions except to state that in his opinion, planning permission would be required regardless if an airfield was licensed or not. Nevertheless, Mr Alston did show interest in the proposals relating to a Wyton airstrip and enquired as to whether it would be available for charter, business and private flying by firms other than Wallace and Jones Limited.

Neville had been reluctant to comment on the Wyton project, fearing he would 'spoil his pitch' if subsequent backing was given to the project by the Hull Corporation as a result of him thrusting an alternative under their noses. Having come this far, he intended to see the issue surrounding air facilities through and hoped the matter would be resolved sooner rather than later. The proposed location of the airstrip was the Wyton Abbey Farm.

Whilst he envisaged a future Wyton airstrip acting as a satellite to a Pocklington aerodrome, Mr Massey, owner of the Pocklington site had tended to regard it as a wholly competitive one. A collect of aviation-minded people had considered Pocklington as being too far out from Hull for light business aeroplanes and would not support the venture for this reason. Neville was content in chipping away at any local airstrip until the Pocklington business had been resolved, praising Mr Massey for being the 'only industrialist in the district to do something instead of merely talking about it'. He believed that there was a definite requirement for Pocklington and other smaller airstrips nearer to the centres of population acting as satellites to a main base. The then prospect of North Sea oil also enhanced the need for an easterly airstrip.

Assuming planning permission was obtainable, it was hoped that a Wyton airstrip would also be available for business and private flying, as well as charter flying by firms other than Wallace and Jones Limited. The whole crux of the matter had been down to planning and Neville did not intend to be 'dangled on a string indefinitely' by the East Riding County Council. With necessary approval, the next step would have been to arrange an overrun east of the airstrip land, enabling its runway lengths to be extended to 1,000 yards or more. He did not anticipate any difficulties in this respect, except perhaps the time in removing crops and grassing the area. It was envisaged the overrun would take place onto the neighbouring Poplar Grange Farm.

Responding to Mr Alston's comments that he had been incorrect in stating unlicensed airfields did not require planning permission, Neville cited a number of unlicensed airstrips which had not received planning permission, including airstrips in Sheffield (Coal Aston) and Scunthorpe operated by the steelmaking, engineering and coal mining company United Steel Companies. He himself had also occasionally used an unlicensed airstrip of over 800 yards, which was based in the East Riding and run by a Mr G. H. Dixon of Skipsea.

At the time the general assumption was that an unlicensed airstrip would have such low air traffic that it would be pointless for a planning decision to be involved, providing no danger or nuisance were caused. However, if an airstrip had a higher amount of air traffic, planning permission would be required but more as a formality than anything else. In order for an airfield to be licensed, regulations stated that planning permission must be granted beforehand. This was to avoid any unnecessary waste of time, say if an airfield were to receive a licence but be refused planning consent later on.

Neville did not feel aviation could be classified under the normal planning rules more commonly associated with buildings. He argued that public amenities such as flying had an intangible quality that had been already fully covered by the appropriate and substantial legislation of the time. A year earlier, the former wartime bomber station at Pocklington had received planning consent for a fairly substantial layout, after being used on an unlicensed basis. Consequently, it was hoped that once the runway had been repaired licensed operations would begin.

There was also a small airstrip operating in Bilton, around five miles northeast of Hull's city centre. At the time, planning approval was being considered for it and it was hoped that the site would be prepared for licensed operations. It is unclear as to what involvement the East Yorkshire Aero Company had with this, but in a letter to Mr Alston, Neville outlined the airstrip in more detail.

The plan for a Bilton airstrip had gone through the Bilton Parish Council and the Holderness Rural District Council without opposition. At an East Riding County Council planning meeting earlier that month, it was also alleged to have been unopposed, but the matter was deferred until a meeting in March to obtain the Hull Corporation's comments. This delay proved annoying but if planning approval was agreed then the airstrip would be in use, irrespective of other sites in the area. He hoped that a decision would go through a Hull Corporation committee meeting in time for March, avoiding further delays.

Due to an apparent existing use right (meaning planning permission would not be required) at the former Hedon airfield, Neville wished to know if the Hull Corporation would be prepared to grant a lease on an amount of the airfield for flying. If so, then he would make a formal application complete with plans for its use. He argued that there was a definite requirement for Hedon in a local aviation network, which he envisaged would include airfields at Pocklington, Wyton, Goxhill and Netherthorpe in Sheffield. The matter of Hedon was considered by a Town Planning Committee on the 12 March and it was decided they would accept the Ministry of Housing and Local Government decision of no flying. Therefore, the request for a lease was not granted and the question of whether Hedon would again be used as an aerodrome remained to be seen.

Away from the world of the planning offices, the de Havilland Tiger Moth (G-ANEJ) aircraft that had started it all was, on the 15 May, written off after turning over onto its back whilst landing in a field at Owstwick, near Withernsea. Although the plane was badly damaged, its passengers Mr John L. Corlyon of Burton Pidsea and the pilot, Ken Charles, managed to escape unhurt. The aircraft had been taxiing across the field when overgrown grass wound around the axles of its wheels, pulling the plane onto its nose and then onto its back. Fortunately, both occupants were wearing safety straps which arguably saved their lives. The plane had not been so fortunate, however, and one of its main plane spars had been badly fractured on impact. Its rudder, fuselage and propeller had also been badly damaged and these defects ultimately proved too costly to economically repair. Whilst the loss of the aircraft proved distressing for all involved, it had been a lucky escape for the two flyers who afterwards counted their blessings.

Around this time, the Hull Corporation had now become members of the Yorkshire Airport Development Association and were also holding talks with the Ministry of Aviation and Hawker Siddeley Aviation. Issues were apparently complex and there were several alternatives being considered by them for the implementation of local air facilities. At a July meeting of an East Riding County Council planning committee, temporary planning permission of five years, subject to approval, was awarded for a Wyton airstrip. This was expected to be in time for an August meeting of the committee and it was envisaged that the strip would be ready for operation by either late August or early September.

Tiger Moth (G-ANEJ) piloted by Ken Charles turned over after landing at Kenby Farm in Owstwick on the 15 May 1965. Inset: Ken Charles (right) alongside John Corlyon, the two flyers involved.

Whilst unhappy with the idea of receiving temporary planning permission with the possibility of having to up sticks once becoming established, it was a question of being thankful for small mercies. Mr Massey had still not made a decision regarding the fate of the proposed Pocklington aerodrome, apparently reluctant to make a move without backing. In Neville's opinion, he would likely obtain more support if he made a move in getting started and if he did, had hoped to combine the operations of both airfields in some way. It was suggested that the proposed Pocklington aerodrome would be an ideal air ferry centre for the whole of the North of England, ferrying cars and passengers between the town and to a part of the continent such as Rotterdam or Antwerp. From experience, Neville suggested that long haul air ferrying would pay well, especially if run as a supplementary service to a sea ferry.

A proposition to convert the Royal Air Force station in the village of Leconfield for civilian aircraft had apparently divided the village on the issue. Neville could not help feeling that the RAF would never completely relinquish the airfield and suspected that the nearby town of Beverley would strongly object to such flying. He suggested that any sudden changes in the Air Ministry requirements could undermine work on the site being carried out by an independent party. Also, if the station was retained for defence purposes, he could not see any realistic joint usage with civilian aircraft believing it was imperative that the RAF take priority at all times. However, the East Yorkshire Aero Company expressed an interest in operating there if given the option to do so.

Neville enquired as to whether the former hangar at Hedon could be made available for Wyton and if so, he would put in a formal request for it. He would never subscribe to the idea of rejecting Hedon after facing difficulties in implementing the Wyton airstrip. Telephone, electricity, drainage and water links at the site were all remote and expensive to install. Hangarage was also non-existent and there would be a battle for more land, essential in making the strip worthwhile. The landowner was apparently unhappy about more of his land being lost to flying. He reiterated that none of these issues would apply at Hedon, which was superior in approaches as well.

Some months after the accident involving the Dornier Do 28 aircraft, Wallace and Jones Aviation had requested Neville's assistance in locating the original invoices and importation documents for parts used on it. This was so they could return remaining spares and settle the matter. Neville had hoped to use the plane on the Wyton airstrip during mid-August, when it was hoped the Ministry would approve the strip for licensed aircraft. He also registered his interest in a Tiger Moth (G-ADJJ) aircraft which the company owned. By August the company, who were now operating as Sheffair Limited, suggested they meet to discuss the two aircraft.

In September, Neville drew the attention of the Hull Corporation to a matter of 'serious concern'. It had been publicised in the local press that a 300-foot cooling tower was to be erected within the Distillers Company factories, in close proximity to the Hedon Aerodrome. The foundations of this were allegedly already completed. As the former Hedon Aerodrome was licensed with the Ministry of Aviation up until the outbreak of the Second World War, he argued that a safeguarding map must be drawn up to protect the airfield's approaches against intruding developments. He suggested that a considerable amount of the existing development at Saltend was already in contravention of these safeguarding agreements.

Evidence of this safeguarding agreement could be found in the minutes of an aerodrome committee meeting in July 1945. Similarly the erection of overhead telephone wires on the former airfield site in 1959 was in contravention of this agreement. After negotiation, British Railways were quite prepared to move the wiring underground should the need arise, but as flying did not take place this need never transpired.

An East Riding County Council planning meeting was to take place on the 9 September in which a decision would be made regarding the fate of a Wyton airstrip. Neville believed that unofficially, approval had already been given but a decision would not be formally made until ten days afterwards. Due to the likelihood of approval, Neville again enquired if the former Hedon hangar would come up for sale in the near future. On the 23 September, planning permission was approved for a Wyton airstrip.

The previous November, Mr Wallace had submitted a planning application for the proposed airstrip at Wyton for use mainly with Dornier STOL aircraft. By the time planning was approved, Mr Wallace had gone abroad and the East Yorkshire Aero Company had the possibility of taking on the lease. The owner of the land had unfortunately passed away that summer. If successful, they felt more land would be required in making a longer east to west run, allowing a wider range of aeroplanes to access the airstrip.

By November a start had still not been made on the Wyton project, with the son of the late landowner deciding not to go through with the proposed airfield, owing to estate difficulties, tenancy renewals and building offers. However, two months later he changed his mind and began negotiating with the flying club on the potential leasing of the land. It was hoped the matter would be cleared up as soon as possible.

Mr Wallace, now flying in the Australian bush, had arguably left the local scene as quickly as he had come into it. Whilst he had the right ideas, Neville felt Wallace had wilted under the formalities which appeared to be necessary to implement flying in Hull. Furthermore, Wallace's former company was no longer interested in flying from Hull. Similarly, proposals had been put forward by British holiday charter airline Autair International for a Hull to Luton air service. Whilst he was in no way against the proposals, he suggested that there would be tough competition from established operators such as British Railways and that Luton would be much too far from London for would-be travellers.

The proposed aerodrome at Pocklington was now under development, although licensed flying had not yet commenced. Neville felt that Pocklington was perhaps the most suitable plot in the area for larger operations, given that planning permission had been approved and an aerodrome licence could be obtained almost immediately. Hangarage at the site was available and he had hoped that an ambitious plan to combine services with the proposed Wyton airstrip would take place, subject to approval.

A meeting regarding the proposed lease on the Wyton airstrip was arranged for the 23 December, with both Neville and Mr Priestman in attendance. Discussions had already taken place surrounding the expenditure involved with such a project and during this it was revealed that the East Riding County Council stipulated improvements be made to the access road. There was uncertainty however as to whose responsibility it was to oversee this work.

DEATH OF AN AIRPORT:

The Hedon Aerodrome Saga

1966

With work still underway in securing a lease for a Wyton airstrip, on the 5 January Neville made another request to the Hull Corporation City Treasurer to purchase the Hedon hangar. His idea was to dismantle the hangar at Hedon, transport it to Wyton and then re-erect it there. The hangar had been vandalised some months prior and it was thought its roof required replacing. Girders had also severely rusted, requiring treatment. Therefore, he believed that it would prove to be of little value to the Corporation. The Territorial Army Association which had used Hedon as a practice ground for many years were also contemplating the relinquishment of it in March of that year. Therefore, he had hoped to be given favourable consideration for it, as a result of his prior dealings there.

By mid-January negotiations were being finalised at Wyton, although the executors of the former landowner's estate were 'driving a very hard bargain'. Along with a rental cost of £800 per year, a premium of £750 was also requested to cover the loss of crops and to allow for the cultivation of grass. Combined with the five-year temporary planning permission and a strip which was smaller than anticipated, the situation was far from ideal. The cost of setting up Wyton as a functioning airstrip would require a considerable amount of capital, with access improvements requiring at least £600 and the installation of fuel storage tanks even more so at £4,000.

Support from various industries and operators both in and outside of the city was noted, although disappointingly backing from the recently formed Hull Business Users Club, which contained companies such as Priestman Brothers, Fenners and Reckitts, had vanished. It was assumed that this was due to their favouritism toward Leconfield. Even so, Mr Priestman had still expressed a great interest in re-establishing Hedon and it was hoped that the former airfield could still be used occasionally for landings. Whilst Neville appreciated this, his efforts in pursuing the re-establishment of the aerodrome had been prevented and consequently his full effort was by now being channelled toward alternative sites.

A meeting between the East Yorkshire Aero Company and landowners was held on the 2 February, in relation to the lease at the Wyton airstrip. A week would pass and it was still unclear if the landowner would grant tenancy. Despite this uncertainty, the club expressed interest over a month later in a Dornier 28 aircraft, owned by Sheffair Limited. The plane would be for business and light charter work from 'an airfield near Hull' and would be used for internal flights, as well the occasional flight to the continent. Provisional figures showed the club would be very hard pressed in making a profit on operations, with the owner of the plane, Sheffair Limited, likely paying it off in a couple of years, whilst the club made a roaring loss due to office expenses and advertising to get the business. Interest was again also shown in purchasing the former Hedon Aerodrome hangar, although this was refused by the Hull Corporation.

Autair International Airways Limited had expressed a desire of operating a scheduled Hull to Luton service and following their application to the Air Transport Licensing Board, a hearing was scheduled for the 5 April. The company had applied for a licence to operate from either Brough or Leconfield

Aerodrome, although the East Yorkshire Aero Company believed that due to the absence of an operational airfield near Hull, their application would be rejected.

Both aerodromes had been perceived as off-limits for civilian aircraft, with Brough having refused multiple requests previously for use of its facilities. Although the East Yorkshire Aero Company had obtained permission to operate there, it had not been possible to persuade aircraft manufacturer Hawker Siddeley to allow the training of new flyers. Neville also felt that Luton would be too far from London to be attractive for potential travellers and although he was not opposed to suitable facilities being provided, there was little chance of this being the case. As such, he intended to personally object to the application.

By now, the East Yorkshire Aero Company was planning to apply for planning permission at a site in the Thorngumbald area, after negotiations relating to the Wyton airstrip project had reached deadlock. The landowner there had apparently refused to grant an option of renewal beyond five years, even though it was thought by all that this option would be included in the terms of the agreement. The landowner had apparently ignored this and despite hopes that negotiations would continue, the strip was then ploughed up and rendered unusable.

Neville felt the whole exercise had been a wasted effort and that he had become something of a laughing stock, following everything that had happened. However, he pledged to get the East Yorkshire Aero Company airborne somehow and consequently submitted an application for a site eight miles from Hull, south of the East Yorkshire village of Thorngumbald. The land in question, Oxgoddes Farm, was owned by a Mr R.N. Leckonby of Holmpton with two adjacent fields to the east owned by a Mr L. Smith of Thorn Barn Farm in Thorngumbald.

In late April, the site was provisionally inspected by the Ministry of Aviation and judged to be the best potential airfield in the area, possessing very flat land and excellent approaches. As there was no hangarage at the site, Neville enquired about the former Hedon Aerodrome hangar wondering if it could be relocated to Thorngumbald. His requested was refused by the Hull Corporation, stating that they would prefer it to be left in situ and 'used in connection with the surrounding area'.

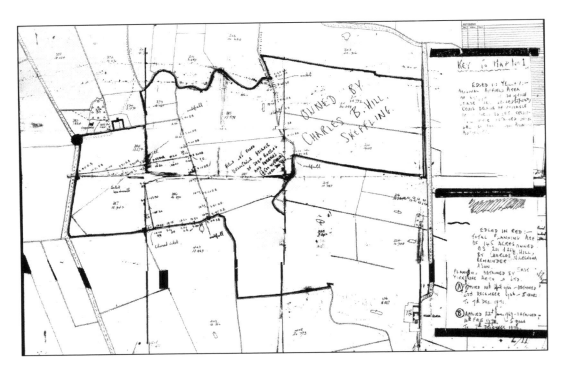

A plan of the Paull site

After receiving a helicopter enquiry from a pilot based in Lincolnshire, the flying club enquired with the Hull Corporation as to whether there were any present or future provisions for the implantation of helicopter landings in Hull. Neville recalled talk of a station being based on the east side of the junction of the River Hull, at Sammy's Point ten years prior. He was informed that some years ago the

Corporation had decided the reservation of a helipad site was no longer justified. This was because, in their view, of the slow commercial development of the helicopter. It was envisaged that operators could occasionally use other facilities when available, although if a number of helicopters wished to land in the city then the situation would be re-examined.

A Leicestershire-based engineer had also contacted the flying club about landing facilities in the city, after apparently being refused permission to land at Hedon. Concerns were expressed about whether the use of Hedon as an occasional landing facility had been withdrawn, although the Corporation stipulated that its use as a landing ground could still be granted, providing it was for no more than 28 days in a year due to planning regulations.

Away from the activities at Thorngumbald, Director of the East Yorkshire Aero Company James Lacey (also known as Ginger Lacey) was featured in the news after being appointed as a technical advisor with famed film producer, the Rank Organisation. The company was planning on producing a film about the Battle of Britain with Lacey, a flight lieutenant and a pilot during the air campaign alongside former RAF pilot Hamish Mahaddie, responsible for the procuring of a full Spitfire squadron. Whilst they had managed to discover 111 of the famous planes, only twelve were said to be in a flying condition. The film was purported as having a budget of around £4 million and was scheduled to be released on the 15 September 1969.

The film aptly titled 'Battle of Britain' was directed by Guy Hamilton and produced by Harry Saltzman, both well established from their work on the James Bond film series. In an interview with acclaimed American film critic Roger Ebert in 1968, Lacey joked that he had 'the devil's time getting the actors to be authentic. I can't get them to cut their hair. In those days, we were all close cropped, and these chaps look like bloody Beatles. They all say they don't cut their hair; they'll ruin their image.' Despite a grand premiere being held at

Leicester Square in London, attended by Her Majesty Queen Elizabeth II, high anti-war feeling spurred on by the Vietnam War and cynicism among post-war generations about the heroism of those who participated in the Battle of Britain, led to the film being dismissed by critics.

Meanwhile at Paull, a planning application had been submitted by the flying club on the 7 November, expressing a desire in using approximately one and a half acres of the land as an airstrip for light aircraft. The land in question formed part of the Oxgoddes Farm and Thorn Barn Farm between Bellcroft Lane and Newlands Lane, about three quarters of a mile south of Thorngumbald. The club anxiously awaited a decision from the East Riding County Council, the authority overlooking the case.

The club had received a few enquiries from aircraft companies, keen on marketing their products. One of these included Beagle Aircraft of Sussex, who had contacted the club about their latest Beagle B.206-S aircraft. On the 8 November, Neville wrote to the aircraft company about aviation progress in the Hull area, revealing how the lid at Brough Aerodrome had come off earlier that year. After Hawker Siddeley had consistently opposed outside use for years, the purchase by Autair International Airways in October possibly had something to do with this, with the holiday charter airline beginning the operation of a scheduled Brough and Luton service. In March, the East Yorkshire Aero Company proudly boasted of being the first company to obtain permission to operate light charter aeroplanes from Brough, although this had not happened for various reasons. One of these being that repeated attempts for permission from Hawker Siddeley to operate a flying school there had been unsuccessful.

Another reason for this was that preliminary investigations had found demand was too little to justify basing even one light charter aircraft permanently at the site. This was very disappointing for the flying club and Neville felt that there was a lot of apathy to overcome before the average person became air-minded.

The Hull Business Aircraft Users Club, which contained three leading Hull-based industrial firms, had at that point chartered a Twin-Comanche from Truman Aviation of Tollerton, whenever an aircraft was required. The East Yorkshire Aero Company had hoped to try and persuade them to purchase an aeroplane and operate it on their behalf. When it was not in use, it would be chartered out to other parties. The East Yorkshire Aero Company had considered demonstrating this plan at some point, but by that time the idea had stalled.

Previously, a trawler owner in Hull had purchased a Cessna 337 aircraft with the intention of building up charter work on this basis. He had planned to use it with his business, basing it at Brough and employing a commercial pilot to operate it. A company was also incorporated under the name of Stellaris, although it is unclear whether any real effort by them was made in obtaining outside work. The East Yorkshire Aero Company, however, intended to follow in their footsteps.

By this time the planned Pocklington airfield had also stalled, with the Hull Corporation apparently not showing their hand on the issue. It was believed that approaches had been made to York Council for potential backers, although rather disappointingly for Neville, he had been unable to persuade the landowner to make even the smallest of starts without backing.

Light aircraft manufacturers Beagle Aircraft Limited were more than willing to bring a Beagle B.206 aircraft to Brough and demonstrate it for the Hull Business Aircraft Users Club. If the club purchased an aircraft, 2½ percent commission would be reserved for the East Yorkshire Aero Company in return for their assistance. The agreement extended to any sale, regardless of who it was. At the time, a new B.206-S aeroplane sold at the price of £41,000, with the lesser B.206 model selling for £35,000. One sale of a B.206-S plane based on the commission agreed would result in £1,025 being given to the East Yorkshire Aero Company for their efforts. Although arguably a small amount, any capital, particularly as much as this, was very much needed.

By December, the Hull Business Aircraft Club was very much interested in the East Yorkshire Aero Company's proposition. Whilst cautious, the wheels were oiled and it was hoped that pressure would be kept up. Even though a sale had not yet been secured, the Aero Company had expressed interest in hiring an aircraft, once they had become airborne, in the hope of securing future sales.

DEATH OF AN AIRPORT:

The Hedon Aerodrome Saga

1967

Early in the year, Neville had been making efforts to revive air services at the former Doncaster airport, discussing the matter with officials from the Doncaster Corporation. Before the Second World War, the airfield in question was once a stopover on KLM's Manchester to Hull to Amsterdam services and he had hoped to use it for business-executive aircraft, charter flights (and if possible) a flying school. During these discussions, he was informed that the area near the town's racecourse was to be redeveloped for housing, although after reconsideration the area was found to be unsuitable due to its risk of subsidence.

The impending £86 million sale of the Distillers Company's chemical and plastics division to British Petroleum raised questions regarding the fate of their Saltend works near Hedon, which produced 200,000 tons of chemicals annually. The company had the option of purchasing another 600-acre site nearby, and only three months prior an executive at the company suggested that they could spend up to £100 million within the next twenty years, developing their current operations into a vast plastics and petrochemicals facility. It was thought that the sale would not have a severe impact on their current operations, quite the opposite in fact, with a spokesman for the company suggesting that the site would have a 'great future' after Britain's entry into the European Economic

Community (EEC). The takeover, in any event, was expected to take place within the next three to four months.

By late January the planned airstrip in Paull was coming to fruition, with planning permission being approved for the site. It was now a case of deciding the length of the airstrip, which it was hoped would cater for the Beagle 206 and 206-S aircraft. It was hoped that the area of the site would be decided in a few days. Telephone installations were also being investigated and existing overhead telephone lines running across the roadside to the west of the airstrip required to be buried, to prevent the westerly approach being jeopardised. On the 25 January, architect and surveyor Mr John Rawdon Binnington drew up plans to install a piped ditch scheme at the newly formed airfield site. This included 1,540 feet of six-inch field drain pipes and 800 feet of nine-inch pipes. On the 5 May, the General Post Office confirmed that the estimated cost of undergrounding the cabling at Paull would be around £320.

Recent research had been carried out by Beagle Aircraft Limited for a customer in mainland Ireland, who had planned on developing a series of airstrips at minimum cost to allow safe operation of the majority of light twin-engine aircraft. Findings showed that at a very minimum, one could get away with around 1,000 yards of distance and anything short of this would severely restrict the types of aircraft able to use it. They concluded that a preferable strip length by their standards would be around 1,250 yards.

By April, proposed plans for the former Hedon Aerodrome had been produced by the Hull Corporation, envisaging that twenty acres of the site could become a road haulage, container services depot and timber storage area. The proposal had already received approval from an East Riding County Council planning committee. Meanwhile at the Brough Aerodrome, Capper Pass and Son, a nearby smelting and refining company, had proposed to build a 600-foot chimney at the site. Predicted to be given the go-ahead, it was thought that the fate of the aerodrome would be sealed as the western end would be completely blocked off by it. Comparative to the former Pocklington Aerodrome, the size of Brough's layout was dwarfed. At Pocklington, there was a choice of three 150-foot runways with the longest being 5,400 feet in length. Additionally, all of the approaches at Pocklington were clear. At Brough, there was only one single 100-foot runway in an area of about 3,400 feet.

By this time, the flying club had begun leasing land at Paull, intending to have it fully operating as an aerodrome by September. The site was considerably nearer to the city centre than Brough and coupled with the fact that the approaches were completely clear and boasting of greater runway lengths, the club had hoped that Brough Aerodrome would wind down their operations once they had begun. Additionally, there was sufficient land at Paull to develop it into a larger airport, adequate to not only meet Hull's needs, but arguably that of the entire Humber.

Neville believed that Autair International Airways had gotten into Brough Aerodrome entirely by chance. Previously, British manufacturers Hawker Siddeley, the company managing the aerodrome, had continuously been opposed to any outside use of the runway until Autair had apparently offered to purchase two of their HS 748 aircraft. Following this, the embargo was quickly removed, thereby allowing the airline to operate from within the aerodrome itself. By now, they were widely advertising their upcoming scheduled air service, due to operate between Hull (via Brough) and Jersey from May until October. Advertisements for the service boasted of journey times as little as 105 minutes.

Neville had not only suggested that Autair were trying to corner the market there with 'no thought for anyone but themselves', but had also never advocated for the creation of a Brough Aerodrome as, in his opinion, the airfield lacked the scope for any sort of development, being hemmed in by a river, a mainline railway, a factory and the village of Brough itself. The irony, in his view, was how it had been suggested that a well established industrial company at Brough be closed down to allow for the expansion of the Brough Aerodrome. Pilots had continually overflown a packed community of around 5,500 industrial workers at the end of Brough's runway and compared to the 1,600 factory personnel at British Petroleum near the former Hedon Aerodrome, these factories were nowhere near the runway.

An advertisement for Autair International Airways, featured in the Hull Daily Mail – 4 January, 1967

The only way of extending the site would be to the left, but this would not provide an alternative runway for the crosswind factor nor would it clear the western end, which was thought to be blocked off by development. On the other hand the proposed airfield at Paull had completely clear approaches and possessed plenty of space for future expansion. Earlier that year, the flying club had tried to establish a flying school at Brough but were unsuccessful in gaining permission. Despite this, the club felt that there was a lack of both suitable hangarage and maintenance facilities there, along with poor accessibility to the airfield owing to the security risk posed by the nearby factories.

In May, after British Petroleum took over The Distillers Company's operations at Hedon, Neville suggested that the oil company had merely picked up their file on Hedon Aerodrome without bothering to dive into the circumstances. Similarly, he felt that all the worriment was more to do with the limiting of its own industrial developments. The club had envisaged using Hedon as a 'close in' terminal, principally for helicopters and short take-off and landing aircraft, the idea being that instead of the public having to go to the service, the service would be brought to the public.

This would allow the airfield to accept more conventional aircraft, whilst also being able to support a heliport in the centre of the city. The view of the flying club was that a potential heliport should be based in the area of Hull's pier, as it was stipulated by the Ministry that any heliport must have water approach. Neville estimated that a helicopter could travel from Hull's pier to a heliport in Battersea, London in just over an hour, cutting the time set by Autair International Airways by at least half. Using American helicopters would have also allowed for a competitive price.

One of Neville's clients had recently purchased a Pilatus Turbo-Porter aeroplane and upon seeing it in action he described it as phenomenal, making the Dornier equivalent 'look rather tame'. He suggested that the plane could easily operate in and out of Hedon, requiring little more than fifty yards in rolling distance, and was convinced that STOL and VTOL were here to stay with the pattern of air transport going in this direction for a few more years. Long runways and vast airfields proved impracticable, especially in a country such as Britain.

In July, the Doncaster Corporation agreed to the provision of an airstrip at the Doncaster Aerodrome, now a shadow of its former self, but deferred the matter until a report estimating the cost of adapting the existing buildings and providing necessary equipment was completed. The East Yorkshire Aero Company too was interested in operating the proposed aerodrome and was negotiating to do this. The civilian aviation division of the Board of Trade was quite prepared to issue a licence for the proposed airfield, with other operators already expressing interest in it over other neighbouring airports such as Castle Donington, Tollerton and Yeadon. This was as the potential aerodrome had a greater density of population and was envisaged to serve towns such as Sheffield, Rotherham and Barnsley. Similarities were drawn with it and the former Hedon Aerodrome, as both were once municipally owned and both happened on the doorstep of their respective cities. They were also similar in that each had once offered the KLM summer service in the thirties.

Neville felt that smaller airfields (or feeder airfields as he called them) would come very much into fashion within the following years, particularly those closer to the centres of population. By this time, large airfields had become renowned for being very expensive to run and usually did so at a loss. With the recent closure of the Hull and Holderness railway line, land north of the line at Hedon with some of the former airfield site could make, in his view, a first class feeder. By August however, the Corporation's view was that Brough had been decided as the first port of call in terms of air facilities to serve the city of Hull, thus ruling Hedon out.

It was now September and the developing Paull Aerodrome appeared to be coming along nicely. Aimed at 'city business executives in a hurry', it was hoped that the airfield would officially begin operations the following month. The East Yorkshire Aero Company had also envisaged using the site for flying training, with its three company directors pouring thousands of pounds into developing facilities at the strip. The site had been granted five years temporary planning permission by the East Riding County Council, allowing the land to be used as a flying club and for charter flying to take place.

The club had been hard at work throughout the year with the arduous task of linking up five fields by cultivating open dykes, as well as building a temporary hangar to house aircraft. Whilst the cultivating work would soon be completed, it would be some months before the club could apply to the Board of Trade for a flying licence. They had hoped to gain the interest of business communities in Hull, arguing that planes as large as those used at Brough could theoretically be used at Paull (although with not as many passengers). At that point, the flying club side of the East Yorkshire Aero Company was being run by Mr Ken Charles who anticipated the airfield would be operating before Christmas. Despite being granted temporary planning permission, the club envisaged they would eventually gain permanent usage of the airstrip.

Behind the scenes the club had spent the past four years negotiating to use the Doncaster Aerodrome, aiming to use it for charter flying, air taxis and a flying school. By October however, they learnt that the lease had been offered to another company. The Doncaster Borough Council had agreed to offer the disused airfield on a ten-year lease at £50 per year to a consortium of local businessmen, who already operated an air service from Yeadon Airport. Whilst the Council's Finance Committee had hoped that both the East Yorkshire Aero Company and the consortium could collaborate in some way, Neville, rather upset about this, sought legal advice after putting four years work into the matter. 'This is incredible,' he told a newspaper reporter, 'these people coming out of the blue.' An architect at the council had tried to amalgamate both companies but to no avail.

The East Yorkshire Aero Company had supplied the local authority with a lot of technical information, taking things stage by stage right through to getting a Ministry of Aviation licence. Neville felt that a condition of any agreement should have been that the consortium could only lease the airfield if they amalgamated with the East Yorkshire Aero Company, instead of 'handing it to them on a plate', as he put it. He stated that 'it is a complete loss of face for us in front of the Ministry of Aviation, after all the work we have put in on it. If we had known we were to be taken for a ride we would not have supplied all the information we did. It is a bad egg all round.' He also argued that £50 a year was a 'ridiculous' figure for the lease of 300 acres of valuable land.

Later in October, the first meeting of the newly formed Hull Aero Club took place, with fifty aviation enthusiasts getting together at the Queen's Hotel in Hull. They had agreed to form a flying club based at the Paull airstrip and it was hoped that members could be given training for £4/10s an hour. This was to be Hull's first flying club since the Hull Aero Club disbanded after war broke out in 1939, with the new club to reuse the Hull Aero Club name. About 150 acres of land was to be available at Paull but initially the club would only use around sixty-five acres, giving a main run of 2,500 feet and at least five hundred yards in any direction. If the club were to use all of the land available, it would give them a total of 4,500 feet for a runway.

Presiding over the meeting was Mr Ken Charles, who stated that within a week or so the airfield would be good to go. At the time, there was a scheme in which flying clubs could hire a small two-seater training plane for £1/15s an hour, although this was not intended as a profit making endeavour. He did not know of any club in the country that offered flying tuition for less than that, with some clubs in the south of England charging around £7 an hour. Even before the war, flying tuition cost less than half of this sum. At the time, the Ministry of Education and Science were offering grants of up to £10,000 to flying clubs and it was hoped that with one of these grants, it might be possible for the club to own a plane.

Interest in membership was already being expressed and by November, a planning application for a hangar and a clubhouse were put forward for consideration. The hangar was to be made of lightweight lattice girders, encompassing transparent corrugated sheets in the roof to allow for daylight. The floor would be earth initially but a concrete floor could be laid in sections at the club's convenience.

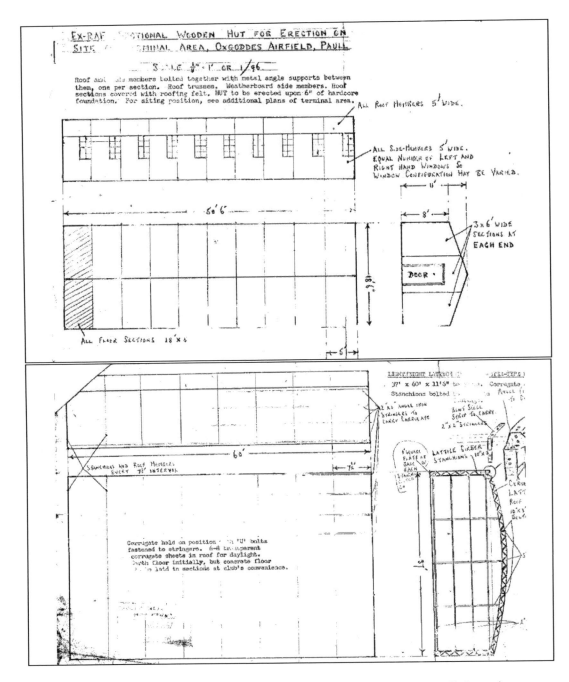

Plans for a sectional wooden hut on site of terminal area – Paull Aerodrome

(6 November 1967)

The provisional plans for the airfield included:

Hull (Oxgoddes) 534225 N, 001050 W AMSL

3 NM SE of Hull, Operational Hours PPO

Grass Airfield 05/23, 2500', 09/27, 2200'

Lighting: Nil.

Hangarage: Nil. Maintenance: Nil.

Restaurant: Nil.

Landing Fee: Not yet agreed.

Remarks: Operated by East Yorkshire Aero Company Limited, as above.

Fuel: On request. Telephone: Not yet connected.

At this point there were too many unknowns to form a useful entry in an airfield directory and the flying club could not give a definite date as to when the strip would be available for use. It was estimated that it would be in operation around springtime the following year because the open ditch culverts, then recently piped between the fields, had not yet all been backfilled with soil. Dependent on the weather, it was hoped this would not take very long.

152

Paull Aerodrome Plan (16 November 1967)

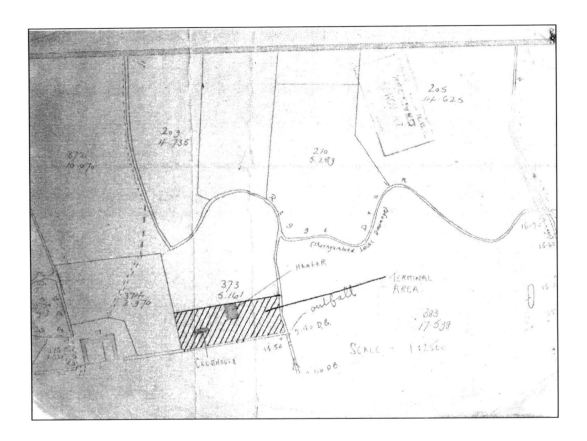

Good news came in December, when planning permission was granted by the Holderness Rural District Council for the erection of a hangar at the site. This permission was only temporary however, and if not extended, would expire in December 1971. If an extension was not granted, work would need to be carried out restoring the land to how it was before the development took place. On the 19 December, it was confirmed that rental of the plot for two and a half years from 1 April 1967 would cost £2,000 a year and then £2,100 on renewal for a further two years, i.e. from the 1 October 1970. Rental for a further five years from the 1 October 1972 would be at an 'agreed' price, but no less than £2,000.

DEATH OF AN AIRPORT:

The Hedon Aerodrome Saga

1968

With permission at Paull now granted, a sense of renewed optimism prevailed in 1968 and it was thought nothing could now stand in the flying club's way. Mr T.E. Richardson M.B.E. was to be made a vice-president of the new Hull Aero Club and vowed to do everything to further the interests and future success of flying in the district. The then newly reformed Hull Aero Club intended to be based at Paull, with the club hoping to open by the spring.

There had been some issues surrounding the lease, with the East Yorkshire Aero Company having to pay out a fee of £2,300, as well as £800 to cover cultivating costs before flying could commence. Cultivation had started very late and whilst the site was level, the surface above the original dykes was flat, bare earth with no grass covering. The club intended for this to be sown down at the end of March or at the very latest, the beginning of April. Whilst the landowner would be in receipt of all this cash without any work required on his part, he had considered putting some money into the project should any become available.

Still, it seemed better to grin and bear it than to go back to Wyton and hope the landowner there would reconsider flying. Beyond this, Neville could not conceive that the Holderness Rural District Council or East Riding County Council would remotely consider approving flying at another site in the East Riding, although if he owned land or knew anyone well enough to contemplate flying, he would follow this path instead. His impression was, however, that the East Riding County Council had pulled out all the stops in approving planning permission at Paull.

In February, Neville made another enquiry about the status of the former Hedon Aerodrome hangar, which by this time had lain unused for a number of years. Despite being rejected in the past, a potentially serious proposition had arisen which he hoped the hangar could be used for. A company were interested in entering light aircraft production in the Hull area, pending the satisfactory completion of negotiations with a southern-based company. It was imagined that they would manufacture a certain type of light aeroplane under licence.

To do this, premises with fly away facilities such as an airstrip would be required. Despite the impending airfield at Paull potentially being suitable, the lack of permanent planning permission would potentially dissuade more permanent investors. As such, he proposed the former airfield at Hedon would be ideal for this purpose. In April Mr G.E. Atkinson, the City Treasurer for the Hull Corporation confirmed that the hangar would not be available for disposal or use, as an application to lease it for a period of years had been considered some months prior.

Neville then enquired as to whether the remaining area of the airfield was available for the placement of a light aircraft manufacturing company, with access from either Stakes or Hull Road. Mr Atkinson confirmed that whilst the Corporation had been granted by the East Riding County Council permission for industrial development on the site, this was limited and referred only to a strip in front of Stakes Road. The company manufacturing the plane parts would need to have them transported to another site for testing, as flying had effectively been banned at the site.

Following the reformation of the Hull Aero Club, its former pre-war chairman and three of its former directors were invited to become president and vice-presidents of the newly formed organisation. Colonel Upton and Mr Richardson had already accepted this invitation, with Mr Clifford remaining. Col. Upton was more famously known as the chairman of Reckitt and Colman, the multinational goods company and grandson of Sir James Reckitt. In May, Colonel Cooper expressed great pleasure in becoming vice-president and it was felt that some of the old traditions of the pre-war club could be recaptured in this way. The unfortunate intervention of war had arguably cut off something which would have otherwise flourished.

In July, Neville contacted British politician and leader of the Hull City Council Sir Leo Schultz, O.B.E. in respect of a newspaper article concerning the subsidisation of losses being made by Autair International Airways. Although it was reported that their withdrawal would result in Hull being without air services for many years to come, the upcoming Paull Aerodrome meant that this was not strictly true, although it was likely that no operator would attempt to run a scheduled service after witnessing the holiday airline's present losses.

Charter services at that time were available from Brough, Pocklington and now Paull to any destination in the UK or continent. Services had been supplied by a number of companies including the East Yorkshire Aero Company, Humber Airways of Grimsby and the East Riding Aviation Company of Pocklington, with all of these aiming to eventually move into scheduled services (although not before routes had been greatly tested first through charter flying). The absence of testing by Autair proved disastrous for the company in terms of losses, but Neville did not feel that these losses should be subsidised. Even if the RAF station at Leconfield were to allow civilian usage, the costs involved in converting the station would prove astronomical. He felt that for the comparatively small amount of capital, £20,000 a year as quoted in the press, a hard runway could instead be financed at the Paull site. At that point, the lack of a suitable local airfield for use had also limited the number of scheduled air services available in the vicinity.

Elsewhere, there was the issue of a potential airport being based at Todwick, with the Conservative Party pushing afresh the case for an airport to serve Sheffield. Whilst there was arguably sense in reserving a site which was available, many argued that such an airport would always remain an airport for light aircraft. Sheffield could not develop a major airport at Todwick alone and the question which remained was whether there would be any substantial demand from local firms for a mini airport. As far as it could be seen, there would be no financial aid coming from either the Government or any authority in the area. Despite Sheffield being the largest city in Europe without an airport, many felt that developing road and rail communications to the full would be a better option, as air operators would likely be more interested in operating at existing airports than starting anew.

Meanwhile at Paull, negotiations were still taking place between the club and the site's owners, with issues arising about who would level the land, as well as a section of land that had been fenced off with large flocks of sheep being placed onto it throughout the day. This had broken the terms of the lease, as permission had not been given to allow any sheep on it during the daytime. The fence would also prove to be a hazard to flying, meaning that some land had been lost for this purpose. Meanwhile, the landowner had apparently prevented workmen from filling a pond in and this resulted in more land being unusable. In Neville's opinion, he felt that they were doing all they could to prevent the club from having full use of it.

Outside of aviation matters, in July Neville had purchased a substantial 200-year-old former vicarage with six bedrooms, in the village of Bilton just five miles from Hull. His purchase had been publicised in a local newspaper after it was revealed that Neville had been sleeping on the floor of the house, which was deserted, in an attempt to deter vandals. Hooligans, thought to be from neighbouring housing estates, had already smashed twenty-five window panes, chopped down trees and stolen various items. With the police investigating, his theory was that by sleeping on the floor there this would be the only way he could stop the place from being smashed up.

The Vicarage, named Swanhill House, stood in its own grounds with an open entrance looking over fields toward the Bilton Grange Estate, which was just a few hundred yards away. He believed that this was where the trouble was coming from as he had previously chased some young boys out of the grounds. He had hoped to move into the house with his wife and three children by the end of the month from his then present home at Ward Avenue, also in Bilton. The damage had followed a spate of vandalism at the nearby Bilton Parish Church, after hay had been set alight and notices were ripped down. Prompt action by the vicar and four of his associates had managed to prevent the blaze from spreading to a nearby oil tank.

Swanhill House, Bilton –1980

Now it was known somebody was in the house, Neville did not expect any trouble and intended to continue sleeping there until his wife and children moved in with him later that week. He believed that the problems began when the East Riding and the York and North Riding police forces merged, as when this happened, a sergeant who had been living in the village was relocated and there was uncertainty as to whether he would be replaced. Despite these inconveniences, it would be a home to him and his three children for the next twenty-eight years. In August, there would be further distress in the Medforth household, owing to the unfortunate passing of Neville's father, Albert. He had been a Director of the East Yorkshire Aero Company for some time and his death came as a great shock to many.

On the 22 August, the Civil Aviation Office visited the newly established Paull Aerodrome and found it to be satisfactory enough to be awarded an aerodrome licence. The following recommendations were made during the visit:

- The main strip NE/SW was satisfactory for length and a width of 300 feet. It was recommended that the corners of the strip be outlined.
- The N/S would need some adjusting to ensure the required width of 300 feet could be reached but it appeared this could be done satisfactorily.
- The site for the hangar appeared satisfactory and at a height of twenty feet the ridge of it must be at least 140 feet from the edge of the N/S strip in order to satisfy the 1:7 side slope criteria.
- It was suggested there would be no controlled airspace problems.

The inspector also recommended improvements to the rescue and medical equipment, including:

1. The appliances must be fully serviceable and capable of being transported to any part of the aerodrome.

2. The principal fire fighting media should be foam and not dry powder or dry chemical.

3. A reserve stock of two 30-gallon fire extinguisher refills and one reserve supplementary agent refill is necessary.

4. All equipment must be protected in boxes or tool-roll and stored on a light truck (an Austin Champ, the civilian version of a British Army vehicle made by the Austin Motor Company).

5. It was preferred that the call to the fire service was earlier than indicated in the list.

6. Contact with the police and fire services were suggested be made.

Whilst work on developing the site was progressing at a steady pace, a licence could not be issued until the recommendations were implemented. A further visit by the Civil Aviation Office was arranged for the 24 October and by that time, planning permission had been granted for the installation of a petrol drum storage chamber.

In November, it was proposed that Mr Ken Charles be made a Director of the East Yorkshire Aero Company. He had been prepared to invest £200 into the company and in the absence of any other capital, this gesture was most welcome. Mr Charles had been Neville's personal friend throughout his endeavours and as he was to be leaving his job, other sources of funding had to be found. Therefore, appointing Mr Charles as a Director seemed to be the most sensible option.

DEATH OF AN AIRPORT:

The Hedon Aerodrome Saga

1969

Twelve years from the initial Hedon enquiries, flying was again taking place at the now operational Paull Aerodrome. All seemed to be going well, with the airfield and its members now established and with no industrial concerns in sight; what could possibly go wrong?

Residents of the nearby Thorngumbald village had begun to complain to the Holderness Rural District Council about the overhead flying coming from the airfield. Indeed, the Clerk of the Thorngumbald Parish Council had himself complained about this. Due to the volume of complaints coming in, the Holderness Rural District Council Committee had no choice but to step in and request that the flying club and its members keep flights over the village to a minimum. It was hoped that by doing this, they would eliminate many of the anxieties which many of the residents faced. The club pointed out however that many of the complaints were of a general nature and there was very little they could do to investigate them.

Whilst the club could recommend exit and approaches, the flight path was ultimately the responsibility of the pilot. The club did highlight how the Paull site was selected due to its sparse locality, with the runway being specifically positioned to ensure it was clear of Thorngumbald. Operators had, by this point, already been requested to avoid the village and the club were unaware that it was being overflown.

A permanent electricity supply at the airfield had still not been installed, although by June a temporary source was being supplied by a generator. The majority of this was being consumed by Bristow Helicopters, the company having taken residence at the airfield within a temporary office. The large amount of electric being used by them was attributed to a number of electric powered heaters being used throughout the day and night, proving expensive for the club.

In May, the Sunday Times newspaper published a report suggesting that nearly two hundred leaders of industry were now using their own company aircraft as an everyday tool of business. Many organisations, including the National Coal Board, major construction firms and several breweries were using such aircraft as a way of increasing the productivity of chief executives, although progress had been 'painfully slow' with the lack of sufficient airfields being suggested as the reason for this. Another problem was the lack of qualified private pilots – around 10,000 in the United Kingdom – and the costs of learning to fly, which were cited as a major barrier. Whilst business flying in America had made a substantial financial impact on the country's economy, the article suggested that the British Government had hampered the growth of light aviation, with the Board of Trade rigidly applying rules to light aircraft, which were in reality intended for large jetliners. Nevertheless, Neville's objective was ultimately to break into this type of flying through Paull.

A planning application to extend the temporary planning permission for a further ten years was submitted on the 20 June. By July, further complaints from the residents of Thorngumbald were being submitted, with one such complaint describing how a small plane crossed over a house at very low altitude. The complainant described how his young son had been woken by the noise after going to bed for the third time that night. This had been the fifth time in the past six to seven weeks that he had been disturbed by these aeroplanes, which had been flying at very low altitudes over or extremely close to the estate.

Following the incident, which took place on the 9 July, the person immediately contacted the police, afterwards travelling to the aerodrome to register a complaint there. Upon arriving at the aerodrome, he met Mr Charles who stated that the offending party was a member of Bridlington Aero Club that had been returning home. Three weeks prior, a plane had also been flying high up over the estate, which cut its engines and proceeded to glide around over the houses in circles.

At around 9.50 pm that evening, Mr Charles excused himself to take somebody up for a 'joyride' as the complainant put it, which finished at around 10.10 pm. He described there being almost 100% cloud cover and it becoming rather dark. The complainant suggested that the licence, issued by the Board of Trade, stipulated there be no night-time flying by the club and that both he and his neighbours had grown tired of the noise being generated by planes every evening and weekend.

Just a few days later, another resident of the village registered the 'strongest possible complaint' in regard of low flying aircraft in the evenings, alongside another who also complained after flying had apparently increased 'tremendously'. He described the activities as coming from a 'privileged obviously wealthy few' who were making life intolerable for the ratepayers of Thorngumbald. Another resident of the village recalled how a learner pilot had cut his engines whilst approaching the landing field and expressed serious worry that if the plane's engine had not 'cut in' again, a serious accident could have occurred to both inhabitants and buildings. Residents also began to worry about their property values being affected as a result of the flying.

By now, 300 complaints had been submitted to the County Council by disgruntled residents opposed to the flying that was currently taking place. Neville expressed dismay over the complaints and felt both he and the club had been fully cooperative when investigating them. He suggested that this willingness to cooperate had been misunderstood as a sign of 'weakness' and also stated that no rules were being contravened by the club. A Non-Directional Beacon (NDB) had been installed south of Thorngumbald which gave off a continuous signal as a navigational aid and had been utilised at all times by both civilian and service aircraft.

Some of the noises reported were, in his view, coming from the RAF, as they had apparently been flying low over the area on patrol throughout the day and night. Despite ongoing negotiations between the Holderness Rural District Council and the club, complaints were still coming in. He felt that the planning authority had to take at least some responsibility in the matter of housing and airfield planning, as the Paull site was originally chosen because of its freedom from surrounding developments. A lot of time, effort and money (estimated at £500) had gone into its establishment.

Developments surrounding other airfields in the area were still ongoing and at Brough, the proposed large chimney in front of the airfield was given the go-ahead, following the completion of an inquiry in August 1967. Whilst still to be constructed, the Board of Trade had still to decide on whether to allow a limited amount of flying when it was finally erected. The decision on whether to continue flying at all was up to aircraft manufacturers Hawker Siddeley, who employed all of the staff that operated the airfield.

With Autair International Airways almost certain to withdraw their services from Leconfield by the end of October, Neville for the first time felt sorry for the company. In his view, whilst they had tried to corner the market, their fingers were 'badly burnt' in the process. By his own account, he had been trying to launch an airfield in a purely private capacity for the past twelve years without local authority support, which had not only cost him his job but seemed destined to break him businesswise. He was doubtful as to whether an airfield could operate without either local authority support or indeed a great number of donors.

The irony, as he saw, was that with just a fraction of the finance allotted to the holiday airline's operations at Leconfield, services to anywhere in the country or the continent could have been provided by his own company instead. He argued that if Hull wanted any sort of air service, the city must meet a private venture for it to continue successfully and on the face of it, Autair did not appear prepared to operate without such support.

Neville's principal customer Bristow Helicopters, which served the North Sea, required more security if it was to remain at Paull. The five year temporary planning permission originally given for the site was due to expire in less than two and a half years and stipulated that unless permission to continue was granted, the land would need to be reinstated to its original condition. The reason for this was to allow use of the land if proposals were ever submitted to develop the north bank of the River Humber. A document entitled the 'Humberside Feasibility Report' regarding future development of the region had been released earlier in the year and made no mention of a dedicated aviation policy for the area. Because of this and as there were no proposals likely to prevent an extension of planning for the aerodrome beyond 1971, a ten year planning extension was applied for with the intention of providing security for both Bristow Helicopters and the Hull Aero Club.

The matter was to go before a planning sub-committee in August, but was deferred until the 11 September pending an inspection of the airfield by the committee. This would take place on the 8 September by two planning officers, with the club offering to demonstrate runway flight paths, the aerodrome traffic pattern and answering any questions put forward by its members. Aircraft were also on standby to demonstrate and take up anybody who wished to view the site from the air. The club also invited members of the Hull Corporation's Planning Department to attend and view helicopters and a light aircraft in action. The presence of aircraft was to demonstrate the flight patterns around the field and the direction of take-off. On the day, council representatives saw Mr Charles fly a bright yellow Condor two-seater plane around the airfield and over the village. A Jet Ranger helicopter, owned by Bristow Helicopters, also took part in the demonstration. Ensuring that the noise levels were acceptable, the representatives watched and listened to the flying from a nearby residential area, calling into one house to watch from a bedroom window.

Neville felt that some responsibility for a local, operational airfield must be taken by both the East Riding County Council and the Hull Corporation planning departments. In his view, the initial five year planning permission was not a commercially viable decision and had potentially jeopardised private investment from people who could visualise no return on their capital in such a short space of time. If the authorities did not wish to support their venture or establish an airfield themselves then at the very least, he argued, they should give the club adequate planning approval in which to make the airfield a commercial proposition for private investment. With all of his own personal capital invested in the project, he was anxious about keeping continuity at the airfield.

In October, an agreement between the East Yorkshire Aero Club and Bristow Helicopters Limited resulted in Bristow purchasing a hangar for £4,350. The hangar was to also include a helipad. That month, the East Riding County Council submitted recommendations to Whitehall for a five year planning extension, after the airfield's runways were slightly reoriented.

Paull Aerodrome Data

(January 1970)

Coordinates – 5342 North, 0010 West

8' AMSL

Operating Hours PPO by arrangement 3 NM South-East of Hull

Grass Airfield 06/24 2350' x 300', 01/19 1650' x 300'

Hangarage and maintenance available

Club facilities available with flying training

Ottringham NDB near 24 thresholds

Fuel available

Maximum potential on present planning area – 3600' East-West, 2700' North-South

In rural setting therefore approaches clear

8 miles to Hull City Centre by road – takes 15-20 minutes.

The Paull Aerodrome site during cultivation – Late 1960s

DEATH OF AN AIRPORT:

The Hedon Aerodrome Saga

1970

In January, a five year extension of planning at Paull was granted beyond the initial run-out day of December 1971, taking it through to December 1976. Around this time, an objection was lodged by the East Yorkshire Aero Company against operator Humber Airways' application for a licence at Brough Aerodrome. Whilst the club did not deny that Brough was more than adequate for the services which the operator had applied for, once the proposed chimney had been completed the runway would likely be put out of action for scheduled operations. According to Capper Pass and Son, the company erecting the chimney, it was to reach at least 200 feet in height by May 1970. Owing to a limited grass area at Brough, it was doubtful a public licence could be obtained from then on.

Its approaches proved problematic as they were already hemmed in by factories to the west, a main railway line, high ground and residential properties to the north, a soon to be erected chimney to the east and the River Humber to its south. It seemed likely that the Board of Trade would issue a 'limited licence' on the airfield restricting larger aircraft, and on this basis the East Yorkshire Aero Club argued that any investment in the airfield was unjustifiable. Their own venture at Paull was unsubsidised and completely private, requiring more capital, more local support and more assurances from authorities with regard to planning and development.

Top: February 1975 Paull Aerodrome aerial view. Shows Blackburn Beverley aircraft on the ground (now at Fort Paull) – [Courtesy of the Hull Daily Mail]
Bottom: Paull Airfield in the late seventies. [Courtesy of Andy Wood – photographer unknown]

In late January, a newspaper article further elaborated on the case for Humber Airways, highlighting how major Hull-based manufacturers Reckitt and Colman had proposed to move its headquarters from Hull to London, due to the lack of a sufficient London air service from the city. This was revealed by the Director of Humber Airways, Mr Jeffrey Fewlass, during a meeting of the Air Transport Licensing Board in London. Humber Airways were asking the Board for authority to operate a scheduled service between Brough and Leavesden in Hertfordshire for tourist class passengers, cargo and mail. They requested the licence be effective for several years, proposing to use Britten-Norman BN-2 Islander and Piper PA-23 aircraft.

Mr Flawless stated that the service Humber Airways had proposed 'would be directly geared to the needs of the business man'. A week prior, the company had done a trial flight from Brough to Leavesden in an hour and five minutes. This was in comparison to the hour and forty-nine minute journey using Autair's service from Brough to London's Euston Station. The Secretary to the Hull Chamber of Commerce, Mr William Hope, supported the application and stated to the Board that 'my council and committee are abundantly satisfied that the proposed service is precisely the kind of no frills service that is likely to meet their own needs'. The only objector present, on behalf of his company and flying club, was Neville.

Whilst questioning the General Manager of Humber Airways, Mr John McKellar, Neville was curious about the effect that the 600-foot high chimney being built at the end of the Brough Aerodrome runway would have. Mr McKellar stated that the chimney, when built, would make it impossible to use the present runway but negotiations were ongoing to solve this problem. Obviously if the runway was to be re-sited, then the chimney would prove not be a hazard and regardless, it would be nine months before it reached critical height.

Neville's objection was over the operator's choice of using the aerodrome itself and not the service being offered, as he could not see it being approved by the Board of Trade once the chimney was completed. Paull Aerodrome, however, had no such disadvantages. He had come away from the Air Transport Licensing Board hearing in January with the impression that there had been considerable discussion between the Hull Corporation, Humber Airways and Hawker Siddeley with regard to their usage of Brough. Although rather unfortunately, cross-examination of Humber Airways staff failed to prove that a licence for public use could be obtained there, once the proposed chimney was completed.

To be sure information was not being withheld, Neville confirmed this with the Board of Trade in Liverpool, who informed him that further airfield data was required from Hawker Siddeley before the matter could be considered. As he was also the holder of a Board of Trade licence, he felt that his company were entitled to object to the proposals. The time had come to officially ascertain what the Hull Corporation's attitude was towards Paull Aerodrome and its future development, in relation to air facilities in Hull.

Having worked out in the open towards the establishment of an airfield in Hull for many years, Neville professed at being somewhat apprehensive about 'closed door meetings'. At Paull, the main hurdle, which had been the temporary planning permission, had been cleared until at least 1976. In comparison to Brough, Paull was nearer to the centre of Hull by road, its runway approaches were 'vastly superior' and its potential for development was greater. Whilst Brough arguably had superior terminal buildings, he felt these were to be of little use if the airfield was to be restricted.

In any event, the facilities at Paull could not be expected to be developed to such a high standard in the short space of time it had been in operation, especially without any guarantees of support from local authorities. It was hoped that Humber Airways would come and use Paull as an operational base and whilst

Brough appeared to be better in the short term, this was assuming a public use licence would be awarded. With the bulk of Hull's industrial developments to the east and the expected increase that way, Neville argued that this would very much bring Paull into the middle of incoming flights, as well as being in an ideal location for air freighting.

With the airfield sixteen miles nearer to northern Europe than Brough, on a turn round distance of thirty-two miles this would inevitably result in lower airfares to and from the continent, where he felt the bulk of air services would develop. Public access was also better owing to Brough possessing certain restrictions due to the close manufacture of military aircraft. It was expected that the use of these facilities would be restricted to the islander type of aircraft and he therefore felt that such expenditure was not justified for such a restricted facility.

Before Brough became 'another Leconfield' with money 'going down the drain', he suggested that a cold, hard analysis be made of both airfields at Paull and Hedon. Being a long advocate of the latter, if there was no intention to support the newly formed Paull Aerodrome in any way, public money would be better spent at Hedon which was also on the city's doorstep. As the former airfield at Hedon was already owned by the Hull Corporation, he argued that it would likely have a greater potential than the Brough Aerodrome would ever have. He also did not think that British Petroleum (BP) would stand in the way of the charter of scheduled operations from Hedon, in the same way The Distillers Company had in 1959.

In April, fire services at the Paull Aerodrome were now being provided by the Kingston-upon-Hull Auxiliary Fire Service Association, whose members were to drive a fire engine when providing the voluntary cover for the Hull Aero Club. The association also hoped to erect a hut at the airfield to house fire apparatus, which had been becoming weathered after being situated outside for some time.

In June, owing to an unfortunate domestic crisis Neville had to abandon all idea of work to care for his children. On the 27 June, an article entitled 'Shattered Dreams of Hull's "Mr Aviation" ' was published in the local newspaper, the Hull Daily Mail. Nicknamed 'Mr Aviation', the article highlighted how he had 'been grounded' after thirteen years of campaigning due to a lack of support, a lack of local authority interest and insufficient capital. This had eventually shattered his hopes of the Paull Aerodrome being the city's future airbase.

He told the newspaper, 'I have tried to run a one man band, but now I realise it was too much for one man to handle. I am on the bottom now. I can only come up again.' His only consolation was that Paull had become an established airfield, but the irony was that nobody wanted to know about it. Developers whom he had approached showed initial interest, but would not consider anything specific until an air firm began running flights from there. 'We have got to have user support before development can take place at the airfield,' he said.

It had been suggested that operator Humber Airways would be unlikely to rush to Paull when the proposed chimney at Brough Aerodrome was completed and there were no other operators in the area for the club to approach. As a result, the 'dreams of Neville Medforth lie scattered over one small chunk of Holderness'. He still believed, however, that Paull was the complete answer to the city's airfield needs and that it had the potential to become a business and executive air terminal providing club facilities, training, a restaurant and an overnight stop. Ambitious plans had been prepared by a London firm of architects the previous October, visualising a country club alongside some light industry on part of the airfield. Rather unfortunately for Neville, he did not have the funds to follow this through.

His withdrawal from Paull also had an effect on the Hull Aero Club, which was consequently tasked with finding £700 a year in rent as well as £300 a year in rates. Mr Charles admitted that what the club needed was someone to help share the load; the field would be an inexpensive airbase with excellent facilities and important radio aids. One way Neville suggested getting over the issue was for a group of local businessmen to get together and fund the project. This, he estimated, would cost between £30,000 and £35,000. 'The income would be small at first, but you could certainly make ends meet,' he told the newspaper reporter. The remaining assets of the East Yorkshire Aero Company, namely the hangar and helipad, had been sold to Bristow Helicopters the year prior. Had this not gone through, he believed that the landowners would have ploughed up the bulk of the airfield. The cost of developing Paull to date was estimated to be several thousand pounds.

SHATTERED DREAMS OF HULL'S 'MR AVIATION'

HULL'S "Mr Aviation" has been grounded. For 13 years company director Neville Medforth has campaigned to get an independent airfield for Humberside. But now, on 145 acres of grass and farmland eight miles from the city centre, his high flying dreams have crumbled.

Lack of support, local authority interest and eventually capital have finally shattered his hope that lowly Oxgoddes Airfield could have been Hull's airbase of the future.

Since 1959 on a variety of airfields throughout East Yorkshire, Mr Medforth has battled against local prejudices, planning authorities and vested interest.

Today, with nothing gained —not even a leasehold on the land he had such big hopes for at Paull—he says: "I have tried to run a one man band, but now I realise it was too much for one man to handle."

"I am on the bottom now, I can only come up again."

THE IRONY

His only consolation is that at Paull he has established an operational airfield.

The irony is that no-one wants to know about it.

Developers he has approached showed initial interest, but would not even consider anything specific until an air firm began running flights from Paull.

"We have got to have user support before development can take place at the airfield," he said.

Today, that support seems as far away as ever.

NEW PROBLEMS

Humber Airways, who face new and costly problems at Brough when the nearby Capper Pass chimney reaches a level to prohibit use of the main runway, are unlikely to rush to Paull.

There are no operators on North Humberside to approach. So the dreams of Neville Medforth lie scattered over one small chunk of Holderness.

Mr Medforth still firmly believes that Paull is the complete answer to Hull's airfield needs.

AIR TERMINAL

It could, he believes, become a business and executive air terminal providing club facilities, training, restaurant and night stop requirements.

Plans prepared by a London firm of architects last October visualise a country club and light industry on part of the airfield.

This takes capital, and Mr Medforth says that he simply cannot afford it.

Although over the years his catalogue of failures is long, Neville Medforth must attract admiration for the fact that he alone has tried harder to establish a north Humberside airbase than anyone else.

STORY BEGAN

The story really began in 1958 when his plans for Hedon airfield collapsed after the East Riding County Council insisted that planning permission was needed. Following objections this was not granted by either the council or Housing Ministry.

After that came plans for Hutton Cranswick airfield, Wyton Bar and Brough.

Finally, in 1966, he turned his sights to Paull and made his first major breakthrough.

Grass runways were laid down and a hanger built—that alone cost him £1,000 — and Bristow Helicopters moved in with their service to North Sea oil rigs.

Paull also became the base for the Hull Aero Club whose members helped Mr Medforth with some of his work.

HULL'S NEEDS

As champion of Paull—it is also known as Oxgoddes Airfield—he sticks with grim determination to the view that it alone can meet Hull's needs of the future.

The view is endorsed by members of Hull Aero Club.

Their secretary, Ken Charles, says that unless an operator moves into Paull, its development cannot get off the ground.

Since Mr Medforth had to pull out, the club is faced with the problem of finding £700 a year rent. On top of that are rates of £300.

SHARE LOAD

"What we need is someone to help share the load at Paull," says Mr Charles.

The field, he adds, would be an inexpensive airbase for Hull. It has excellent approaches and important radio aids.

Mr Medforth says one way of getting round the under-capitalisation problem would be for a group of local businessmen to get together and help start the ball rolling.

This would take £30,000 to £35,000 on his reckoning.

"The income would be small at first, but you could certainly make ends meet."

So for the moment the whole thing rests. All Neville Medforth can now hope for is to be proved right sometime in the distant future.

Shattered Dreams of Hull's 'Mr Aviation' – Hull Daily Mail, 27 June 1970

Despite this seemingly devastating news, Neville remained enthusiastic about the need for an air service to serve the city of Hull and with Paull no longer an immediate cause for concern, he began exploring other avenues. In September he wrote to the Lord Mayor, who was also Chairman of the Hull Regional Development Committee, advocating the cause for the aerodrome. Again in October, Neville revealed that the Paull Aerodrome 'project' was going ahead, with potentially adequate capital available to allow for the purchase of the airfield and its immediate surroundings.

Over 4,000 feet of runway with almost 3,000 feet of subsidiary distance was hoped could be made available by 1971, with planning consent on all of the land secured. There was potential in the area to allow for ample scope to extend the airfield by around 6-7,000 feet. Land not in use for aviation, it was hoped, could be redeveloped as a light industrial estate, to allow for the subsidisation of airfield operations. With the need for new light industry in the area to provide suitable employment opportunity, he could not visualise opposition on planning grounds and the financial responsibilities on the airfield would be greatly relieved.

At the end of October, a Hull Corporation Regional Development Committee had agreed, as an interim measure, to assist with the provision of a civil air service from Leconfield until the 31 March 1971, alongside operator Humber Airways. The Town Clerk of the Corporation insisted that their interest was to maintain, if possible, a civil air service for the area and that further negotiations would be held with operators in the New Year. Any further support by the Corporation would depend on these talks. The provision of Leconfield as the city's airbase, Neville believed, was a short-sighted policy and that Hull must have an airfield available for general use and round-the-clock operation if demand necessitated it. It was this belief that had founded the project at Paull and he could not see Leconfield meeting Hull's needs. He was also disappointed that his company had not been offered an interview by the Corporation regarding the envisaged development of Paull, with no committee members having visited the site, as far as he was aware.

DEATH OF AN AIRPORT:

The Hedon Aerodrome Saga

1970s

The activities of the East Yorkshire Aero Company slowed down somewhat during the decade, with Neville directing his energy towards his childrearing responsibilities. Nonetheless, the Hull Aero Club continued to operate at Paull and in June 1971, an air display of The Barnstormers was organised by Mr Charles and staged at the airfield. The event was such a success that it was decided it be an annual occurrence. Tragically just over a year later, Mr Charles was killed during a flying accident in August 1972 at the Burton Constable airfield, with many of his colleagues witnessing the disaster. The club's chairman at the time, Mr Jack Ross, wrote to each member saying 'Ken lived for Hull Aero Club' and a tree was subsequently planted at the site where Mr Charles lost his life.

During successive years, the Hull Aero Club continued to grow and on 30 March 1974, a Blackburn B-101 Beverley aircraft (XB259) landed on the airfield in what would be its final flight. The aircraft, now the only one in existence, it was hoped could prove to be a popular attraction, although unfortunately this did not come to pass. In December 1976, a planning application was submitted to continue usage of the airfield. Despite this being granted, in 1981, little over ten years after its founding, Paull Aerodrome would cease its operations and the Hull

Aero Club were forced to set up elsewhere. In April 1983, after the airfield had closed, the Beverley aircraft would be moved to the Museum of Army Transport in Beverley, East Yorkshire and eventually to Fort Paull.

Air displays at Paull – **Top**: 7 July 1975 **Bottom**: 11 July 1976

[Courtesy of the Hull Daily Mail]

In March 1974, an article published in the Hull Daily Mail highlighted how a regional airport for the Humberside area was to be developed on the south bank of the estuary, midway between Grimsby and the south end of the Humber Bridge, at Kirmington Airfield. It had been proposed to the Humberside Planning Committee that the official title for the airfield be 'Humberside (Kirmington) Airport'.

The decision to develop the former wartime airfield as the area's main base for civil flying came after years of searching for suitable sites on both banks. It was said that if the airport attracted operators of package holidays, allowing residents of Humberside to use it instead of travelling long distances to an alternative airport, then the county was likely to be favourable towards it. Nevertheless, hesitancy about pouring big money into the project was expressed as many argued that it was primarily for a minority. In January 1974, the Planning Committee allocated £80,000 for the 1974-75 running expenses of the proposed Humberside Airport.

Chairman of the Committee, Councillor Alex Clarke of the Hull Corporation, made known that the proposed airport would be the main airfield serving Humberside. The decision to develop the airfield in 1972 had been taken by the Lindsey County Council and now Humberside were to take up where they left off. Previous attempts at locating a site on the north bank for development as a regional airport had proved unsuccessful, with thousands of pounds being spent by the authority on the Brough and Leconfield Aerodromes. Still, passengers and businessmen from the area would be inconvenienced in getting to Kirmington until the completion of the Humber Bridge in 1981, with the site being situated thirteen miles from Grimsby and seventeen miles from Hull.

The Committee had envisaged the airport as a regional one, mainly carrying passengers between Humberside and London. It was not considered that it would be one used for international flights. In late 1972, the Lindsey County Council had agreed to a £250,000 scheme in converting the former RAF bomber station and whilst recent orders had requested that local governments cut down drastically on expenditure, it was not anticipated that the money for the development would be withdrawn.

Their decision to agree on the scheme had followed a £70,000 contribution from the British Steel Corporation made towards the development costs of converting the site. This was in return for a five year concession in using the airport. In late 1973, the Lindsey County Council agreed on a £150,000 contract with International Aeradio Limited, for the company to manage the airport. By 1974, the airport was being used extensively by aircraft carrying business executives to and from the Humberside area, air charter companies and a flying school.

With the Humberside Airport now established, the Director of Industrial Development at the Hull Corporation, Mr Ian Holden, had likened the city to a sleeping giant that was quietly awakening. The comparison had been made at an annual conference of the Institute of Traffic Administration in October 1975, during a talk entitled 'Hull – a City of Change and Opportunity'. The talk focused attention on the city's future and potential for development.

Despite being the twelfth largest city in Britain, Mr Holden had highlighted how change in Hull had not been as dramatic in terms of its road network comparative to other cities. Influencing this change was the potential growth of European Trade, with the predicted development of the European Economic Community (EEC) in the coming decade. It was hoped that this, together with the M62 motorway, would assist Hull as a future commercial centre. The EEC would arguably also bring about the potential for future aviation development, something that Neville had predicted more than twelve years prior.

Around the same time the development of a bridge across the Humber, something which many in the surrounding areas had worked for more than a hundred years to achieve, was finally bearing fruit. Aptly named the Humber Bridge, it was designed to link both areas either side of the estuary and it was hoped that it would eventually prove to be the key towards future development in the then county of Humberside. Previously, communication between both sides of the river had proved somewhat difficult and it was estimated that road journeys between the two sides would be cut by as much as fifty miles. Prior to the bridge being built air travel had been a popular way of combating this problem, although with the creation of the bridge, easy access was now possible by those situated north of the Humber to the then newly created Humberside Airport. This, some may say, further eliminated the need for an airfield located near the city of Hull.

The whole development was made possible through the Humber Bridge Act of 1959, which had been endorsed by the Hull Corporation and was passed to allow for the creation of the Humber Bridge Board. This was composed of representatives of the Corporation, the East Riding County Council, the Lindsey County Council, the Scunthorpe Corporation and the Urban District Councils of Barton-upon-Humber and Haltemprice. The Act gave the Board necessary powers to construct a bridge, including the authority to acquire the necessary land to do this and to allow the borrowing of money to fund the development. Further powers were granted allowing the Board to operate and maintain the bridge once it had been built, including the power to take tolls from its users.

In May 1971, the Minister for Local Government and Development announced in Parliament that the creation of the bridge was to go ahead, with central Government lending the Board 75% of the costs to do this. This would be repaid through tolls. Just over a decade later on the 17 July 1981, the bridge was officially unveiled by HM Queen Elizabeth II.

DEATH OF AN AIRPORT:

The Hedon Aerodrome Saga

1980s

In March 1978 the Environment Minister was to decide on the future of the Paull Airfield, after the Ministry of Agriculture had objected to the landing of aircraft for an unlimited period. Indeed, this would eventually see the closure of the aerodrome in 1981 and with the establishment of Humberside Airport in 1974, the aviation scene within the Humber area would remain largely unchanged. Perhaps Hull Aero Club's swansong at Paull was their display celebrating the fiftieth anniversary of Amy Johnson's solo flight to Australia, in May 1980. Earlier, they had marked the fiftieth anniversary of the opening of the former Hedon Aerodrome, a location from where Johnson had famously flown, with an event which included a low flypast by four light aircraft on the 8 October 1979. The aircraft taking part were Cessna 150s G-AZID and G-HULL, Cessna 172 GAVZV and GA7 Cougar G-BIIBC.

Despite opening in 1968, the facilities at Paull had never really been developed to a high degree of sophistication. The Hull Aero Club had, however, arguably done its best to encourage business users through the installation of night lighting and approach aids. Additionally, Paull was still the only airfield in the region at the time licensed by the Civil Aviation Authority in handling air transport movements, regularly serving such twin-engine aircraft as Aztec, Duke and

Cougar. During their annual air show the previous year, the short-haul airliner de Havilland Dove, commonly used as a regional jet, had been the second heaviest plane to ever land at Paull. It was through these ventures that those behind the Hull Aero Club had hoped would encourage those in business to take advantage of the airfield, although rather unfortunately this was not to be. Despite ever increasing numbers of people travelling by air, both recreationally and on business, airlines faced a gloomy immediate future with sharply rising costs. One correspondent suggested in March 1980 that the 'cheap-fare revolution (was) ending'.

For a period of time after 1981, the Hull Aero Club would be based in Bridlington, Brough and ultimately Leven where they continue to be today. Despite being forced to leave Paull in 1981, the Hull Aero Club's annual air show still went ahead, being sponsored by a national newspaper and staged at Humberside Airport the following July. The highlight of the show was said to be a top flight aerobatics competition with a trophy and big cash prizes.

Six leading British aerobatic pilots, including champion Mr Philip Meeson, were to take part. Mr Meeson would later be known as the Chief Executive of Jet2.com, one of the largest scheduled airlines in the country, based at Leeds Bradford Airport. Two premier Royal Air Force display teams, the Red Arrows and the Falcons Parachute Display Team, were also to lend their weight, with the event expected to be one of the biggest of its kind in the north. Eastern Airways, Humberside Airport's own airline, were to also give their full backing to the show. The display had been organised by Mr Peter Willoughby, who had been involved with the annual air shows whilst at Paull.

Still wishing to keep a hand in aviation, in March 1983 Neville wrote to the Department of Industrial Development at the Hull City Council, arguing the case for Hedon Aerodrome. It had now been twenty-six years since his initial attempts at establishing a flying school there and once again he hoped to gain possible use of the former aerodrome for light aircraft. He expressed disappointment when the department 'cooled' in their responses to him, but he was still very much passionate on the subject of local air facilities for a city of 300,000 inhabitants. In November 1986, Neville again enquired if the possibility existed for assistance in the purchase of the Hedon site, either in the form of a loan or a grant, for the purposes of flying. It is unknown as to whether any possibility towards this was shown.

Although with other matters diverting his attention, including the somewhat short-lived motor racing career of his son, he began to turn his attention towards helicopters and in June 1987 expressed interest in a site to the east of Alexandra Dock on the River Humber waterfront. This was so far as to request the appropriate planning application forms, together with a notice for service on the landowner. In August, he proposed an idea for a riverfront helicopter base where approaches over the water could be made. Rather unfortunately for him, a public footpath stretched along this which somewhat hindered these plans.

Previously the Liberal Councillor John Bryant, who was on the board for Humberside Airport, had attempted to put forward the idea of a Hull helicopter link with the then upcoming airport at Kirmington. Whilst aviation chiefs at the time suggested that there would be nothing to stop the city from having its own heliport, they warned that the project may end in commercial disaster. An attempt at installing a private heliport in the city a year earlier had caused a torrent of protest and eventually was refused by the planning committees.

A landing area on the site to the east of Alexandra Dock would need to be inshore from the bank, although how much so was unclear. It had been suggested to him that a system of hooded traffic lights either side of the footpath running along the approach area, along with warning notices, be used. At any rate, helicopter movements would be on a prior permission basis so that adequate warning and protection could be given to the public. There was a fence near the footpath that could provide some protection, however this required some repair. The landowners, Associated British Ports (ABP), were also aware of the idea and insisted that the whole area be fenced off should the development take place.

The Civil Aviation Authority was less concerned however about the public footpath issue compared with the Hull City Council, sentiments shared by a local helicopter operator. After visiting the site, Neville professed to not seeing anybody using the footpath, instead seeing only one or two fisherman near the channel of the Holderness Drain where it joined the river. On this basis, he felt that the footpath must be put into perspective and not blown out of proportion. Whilst a fence guarding the path throughout the length of the foreshore did impose a restriction on the movement of helicopters, Neville intended to dismantle this.

In September 1987, the Civil Aviation Authority suggested that an ideal solution to the footpath issue would be to re-route it to the north and remove the two-metre wooden fence which could cause an issue. Alternatively, the footpath could remain with suitably positioned notice boards giving adequate warning to anybody using it. Neville was recommended to persist with the aim of keeping the manoeuvring area over the water, as whilst there was a clear overland approach, should ABP develop the adjacent areas he would have found himself in trouble with obstacles of great height. Additionally, as ABP were insisting on having fencing in place, this would potentially have caused problems with the land-based manoeuvring area.

In October of that year, ABP confirmed that land to the east of Holderness Drain as far as Corporation Road would not be available for use as a heliport, due to its potential for future cargo handling activities. Access was also poor and the company could not contemplate installing road access from Alexandra Dock via the drain bridge. Island Wharf was also unavailable due to its current usage and its potential for redevelopment. With the port operator's recent sale of the

Victoria Dock site to the Hull City Council, there was the possibility of the council including a heliport in their redevelopment proposals for the site.

As far as Alexandra Dock was concerned, the site at the SE corner remained the only viable area which the company could consider for this use. Although ABP requested the riverside fence remain, they had no control over the public pathway and it was likely this would have to remain as well. The company could not see anything less than two acres being used for either one or two helipads and consequently requested rent of £10,000 a year. Any work necessary in bringing the heliport into operation, including the connection of services by ABP, would have to be met by Neville. The operator implicitly stated that they would not be prepared to support his proposal in any other way, except on the basis of providing land and services in a commercial sense.

Meanwhile, Neville's dearly loved Tiger Moth (G-ANEJ) which had long since been unused was in the process of being put on the market. Its registration had been annulled many years prior in September 1973, when it was 'Presumed Withdrawn from Use'. However, the selling process would not begin until early 1987 and eventually, two years later, it was sold in February 1989. The day prior to its departure, he spent the whole day cleaning the aircraft in an outbuilding, recalling his time collecting it in 1959 with great affection. Many years later, the plane would become an exhibit in the Royal Malaysian Air Force Museum (RMAF).

187

The Tiger Moth (G-ANEJ) being prepared for sale at Swanhill House, Bilton (1989)

The Tiger Moth (G-ANEJ) in the Royal Malaysian Air Force Museum, Kuala
Lumpur – 2009

[Courtesy of Dr Frikkie Bekker]

In February 1989, a decision on whether financial assistance to allow proceedings with the proposed residential scheme in Victoria Dock was being awaited. Eventually, no support would be forthcoming from either the Hull City Council or any other sources and Neville felt that the chance for a heliport in Hull had been lost. In February of that year, ABP agreed that whilst the land at Alexandra Dock was still available, this would likely change if the company were to develop along the riverfront.

In particular, a new berth to the west of the King George Dock entrance would bring shipping very close to the SE corner of Alexandra Dock and a new radar mast would also be well to the east of this area (opposite Queen Elizabeth Dock). The port operator was adamant that these developments would be given priority over a helipad, with the view of securing a long-term future for the port. It is worth noting that as part of the *Green Port Hull* development in the city, the proposed construction of a wind energy machine manufacturing plant at Alexandra Dock would see a helipad being installed on the site alongside offices, warehousing, external storage areas and a wind turbine of up to 6MW. The facility is expected to become operational between 2016 and 2017, thirty years after Neville's initial enquiries.

Alexandra Dock, Kingston upon Hull (June, 1985)

DEATH OF AN AIRPORT:

The Hedon Aerodrome Saga

1990s

Now in his seventies, Neville's activities slowed down somewhat but he still managed to keep his finger on the pulse in regards of aviation. He showed great interest when the former Hedon Aerodrome once again made an appearance in the local press in May 1990, following a meeting of the Hedon Town Council Planning Committee. The main item for discussion had been a proposal submitted to the Holderness Planning Authority by a local businessman and member of the Holderness Borough Council for Burton Pidsea, Mr Peter Read. Mr Read, who had already built and was extending a hotel on the outskirts of Hedon, had submitted plans for the development of the whole former aerodrome site, which was still Hull City Council owned.

He had managed to obtain the plot on which he built his hotel, alongside the roundabout at the start of the Hedon bypass. Now, he had plans for the whole field, extending from Hull Road to the former railway line and from Staithes Lane to the town of Hedon itself. A map, which was attached with the article, showed readers the extent of this piece of land and its position between Hedon and the industrial belt at Saltend.

Mr Read had initially planned to develop an eighteen-hole golf course on the majority of the land, amounting to 130 acres, but insisted that this would only be possible with the addition of other developments to finance it. A package, including the building of a business park over 34 acres bordering Staithes Lane, a residential development of two hundred houses across 22 acres at the eastern end of the field and a short stay caravan park opening onto Hull Road between the Glencoe Villas, was submitted. The remaining six acres would potentially serve continental ferry traffic.

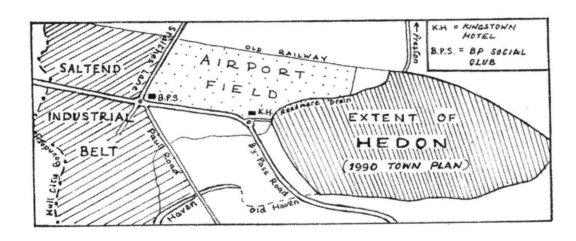

He had first submitted plans for a golf course in 1980, which were approved, but since then the businessman had found it impossible to finance the project. Instead, he had built a hotel in place of the clubhouse. Whilst he argued his new scheme offered housing, work and recreation all in one, the Hedon Town Council opposed the plans which, despite being on land outside of Hedon, suggested would have a great impact on the town. It had never been planned to extend Hedon beyond the Reedmere Drain (its NW boundary) since medieval times and therefore the council could not support the planned housing development.

They had also never backed any extension of the industrial belt across Staithes Lane toward the town and so similarly could not support his plan for industrial units. Then Mayor of Hedon, Councillor Hilda Ives, revealed their dissatisfaction towards the proposed caravan park, which would be adjacent to the BP Social Club. With traffic congestion at the Saltend roundabout likely to cause issues, it was argued that the caravan park would distract from the historical approach to the town. Whilst the council expressed no objection to the establishment of a golf course on what they considered to be a green belt, they were against the rest of Mr Read's proposals. The general worsening economic climate proved somewhat of a factor in their reluctance towards the project, although opposition to a proposed waste incinerator near the site only further influenced their decision. With the matter to go to the Holderness Borough Council for consideration, Neville felt that the Hedon Aerodrome greenbelt should be preserved at all costs.

In 1987, a new international aerodrome known as the London City Airport was established in London. Commenting on the airport in 1990, Neville argued that it had less space than the former Hedon Aerodrome in its prime and expressed dismay toward the notion that the whole of the civil aircraft industry had been sold out to the jumbo jet and large airport concept. This was not a trend that inspired him.

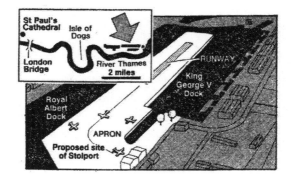

London City Airport (1987)

A newspaper report published at the time revealed how the proposed mini-airport was to open after Government approval, with the decision being promptly condemned by the Greater London Council in spite of strict conditions imposed limiting nuisance to residents in the surrounding area. Work was to start immediately on the former Royal Dockside in Newham and it was envisaged that more than one hundred daily flights for the city's businessmen, departing to Paris, Brussels, Frankfurt, Rotterdam, Amsterdam and nine British cities would be provided using fifty-seat airliners. The airport was to be built by one of the largest construction and civil engineering companies in the country, Mowlem, at a cost of £12-15 million.

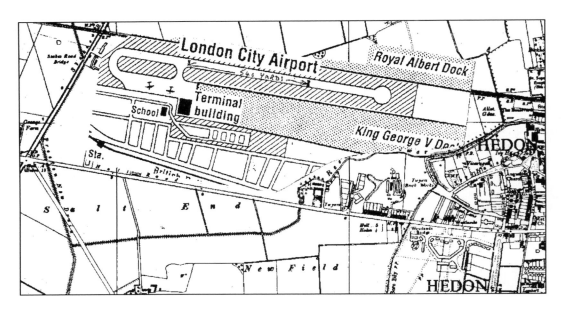

Neville pasted a plan of the London City Airport over the site of the former Hedon Aerodrome, demonstrating that it would possess adequate space for such a development.

In January 1994, Neville expressed shock that recent developments in Hull had not included provisions for a heliport. Furthermore, it seemed to him that every square yard of riverfront had been earmarked for purposes on an 'anything but' basis. He had been prompted to write in to the Town Clerk about this matter, after reading a recent press report concerning the purchase of Sammy's Point by the Hull City Council from Associated British Ports (ABP) for a figure in excess of £1 million. Helicopters with a capacity to land anywhere were obviously at their best when operating on a point to point basis and it was both impractical and unnecessary, he argued, to place a heliport miles from the centre of population. The general layout of Hull resulted in approaches having to be made over water, so as to avoid overflying built-up areas and this was a view endorsed by the Civil Aviation Authority.

A confidential report on this subject had been prepared forty years prior by the Hull Corporation's Town Planning Officer. In fact, as far back as 1952, a Town Planning Committee had discussed helicopter services and sites for the city, with Sammy's Point found to be the most suitable out of all the sites suggested in the report. Neville was similarly astonished that the forward thinking exhibited by City Fathers more than forty years ago did not seem to be shared by the present authorities. These days he argued, there is often a great shout about various projects that will turn Hull into a boom town, although unfortunately, none of these schemes include air facilities.

Disappointed that none of the representatives in Hull seemed to be remotely interested in the idea of a city heliport, he still felt that there should also be the provision of a business airstrip for fixed wing aircraft, close to the city. He argued that any individual or group can produce a scheme for yet another residential precinct or supermarket on every conceivable open space, because in this age of so-called developers, 'a fast buck can be made'. He suggested that the word 'aerodrome' had become almost a dirty word and refused to refer to the vast airport complexes and jumbo jet package tours with it. Instead, he only referred to smaller airfields for use with smaller aircraft which, in his view, had become a neglected side of aviation.

Neville objected to the idea of any development at the former Hedon Aerodrome site for either housing or a golf course, as he argued there were already thirteen established courses or driving ranges listed in the telephone directory at the time. A fourteenth was being constructed at Howden and a fifteenth had been proposed in Hedon. This was compared to only two flying schools in the area, an activity which he also saw as recreational. After the closure of Paull Aerodrome in 1981 and the subsequent relocations of the Hull Aero Club, he argued that golf clubs would not be expected to be shunted around from 'pillar to post' so why should airfields. It was now May 1995 and after years of campaigning, there was still no operational aerodrome for light aircraft in the Hull area.

In September 1996, Neville submitted his views as part of a City Development Plan administered by Hull City Council, arguing that aircraft (fixed wing or helicopter) were quite useless without somewhere to operate and suggested there was a marked reluctance by the local authorities to consider facilities such as helipads and airstrips. He felt that if the Hull City Council themselves did not wish to provide these facilities, then they should not stand in the way of anyone who did either through planning or in any other way. If the local plan inquiry was concerned with land use, then he argued that for fifty years the Hedon Aerodrome site had been squandered.

At the time most of the provincial airports including Kirmington and Yeadon in Leeds possessed flying schools, so he wondered why Hedon had been stigmatised. He felt that the power politics involving big companies and local authorities should have had no part in suppressing air facilities, suggesting that after his company's demise at Hedon in 1961, the back door 'flew open' and business aircraft operated by large companies began to use it.

The Hull City Council disagreed with Neville's consensus, as in their view the use of helicopters by the general public had not developed as envisaged in the early fifties. In a document prepared by Mr C.A. Cumberlin on the 26 September, he argued that the Humber Bridge had been built since that time to cater for road journeys across the estuary and Humberside Airport had been developed to serve the air needs of the Hull, Grimsby and Scunthorpe areas. There was no indication of a further need or demand for such air facilities and whether these could be substantiated.

He suggested that identifying suitable sites for a heliport or airstrip within or close to the city would prove extremely difficult, and with regard to Sammy's Point, as the site was adjacent to housing it had also been allocated for this use. As the former Hedon Aerodrome was outside of the city's boundaries, it was therefore outside of the area covered by the Hull City Council. Mr Cumberlin also suggested that any proposals within the area would likely raise concerns regarding noise, safety, atmospheric and other environmental pollution, and additional questions would potentially arise regarding the demand for and viability of such facilities, as well as who would finance them. For these reasons, the Hull City Council deemed it inappropriate to allocate a site for a heliport or airstrip.

So after forty years of effort, the prospect of re-opening the former Hedon Aerodrome was shattered. That same year, Neville moved out of his Bilton home after twenty-nine years and began a new life in Hull. His final days would be spent writing his book and caring for his children and grandchildren. On the 13 January 2007 after suffering a minor stroke, he was admitted to Hull Royal Infirmary for a short rest over the weekend. A day later, he fell whilst in the ward and broke his hip, proving to be the catalyst that would see his health rapidly decline. He died on the 8 July 2007 at the age of 82.

Neville's passion for aviation appeared to be unmatched. He had met with the American First World War flying ace Eddie Rickenbacker during a conference at the Brough branch of the Royal Aeronautical Society in 1968. His idol was aviation hero Amy Johnson and he was a member of the Amy Johnson Appreciation Society (AJAS) between 1993 and 2003. In 1993, he decided to write a book about his experiences, but found it difficult to find the time due to his health. In spite of this, he began the long process of writing his book which he was doing right up until the end. During the final years of his life, he worked alongside Eduard Winkler of Hedon (or Ted, as he is better known), a local history author behind works such as 'A Civilian Affair', a book charting the history of the former Civilian Aircraft Company.

Mr Winkler's own experiences of the Second World War proved less than ideal. After serving as an armourer as part of the Luftwaffe in 1942, and following recall to Germany in the summer of 1944, he was captured on the banks of the Rhine on the 2 March 1945. Brought to England as a prisoner in 1946, he was finally released on New Year's Eve 1948 and has remained in East Yorkshire since. Whilst both fellows had hoped to publish a book on the history of the aerodrome, Neville's untimely passing sadly meant that he would never see it finished. Nevertheless, the information he meticulously researched and gathered would ultimately prove useful for the creation of this book instead.

The next section has been compiled using various different pieces of text written by him throughout the years.

Prologue

A Hull visitor unfamiliar with the city might arrive by train at Paragon Station in the town centre and then decide to have a look at the east coast, perhaps heading for the small seaside resort of Withernsea, which was recently visited by Prince Charles.

For this destination, it is a simple matter of boarding an East Yorkshire service bus at the bus station adjacent to Paragon. Within a few minutes travel, the main eastbound road out of Hull known as Hedon Road will be reached, a long straight road taking us past various industries on both sides, especially the large Alexandra and King George docks to the south.

Slightly further on, the huge industrial complex at Saltend may be seen with the British Petroleum chemical plant being the largest.

Just beyond here to the north of the Saltend crossroads, there is an unusually large open expanse of grassland comprising of around 200 acres. The clue to its origin lies alongside the road where a rather old battered-looking garage stands. Somewhat incongruously, the lettering above the doors reads 'airport garage'. With a cursory glance, our Hull visitor might ponder as to why only a few grazing sheep may be seen on what is now obviously an aerodrome site with not an aircraft in site.

After returning from the east coast outing with curiosity aroused, the visitor might enquire about the airport garage and the derelict airfield beyond. Anyone old enough to remember would reply: 'Oh yes, Hedon Aerodrome. That is where the Hull municipal airport was. They used to manufacture light aircraft in the long building behind the garage in the early thirties.'

The next question as to the whereabouts of the present Hull airport might receive the reply: 'There is an airport at Kirmington across the River Humber, about twenty-five miles from here over the Humber Bridge.'

By now, our Hull visitor might wonder why you have to go such a long way across the Humber when there is a local airfield on Hull's doorstep right here.

The writer will attempt to recount the details of this incredible saga which most certainly kept him out of a career in civil aviation. It should also answer the query – just what did happen to Hedon Aerodrome?

(A.N. Medforth – 2006)

The Hedon Aerodrome, taken during the 1930s

[Courtesy of the Hull Daily Mail]

1.

The Beginning

It is now over 100 years since the Wright Brothers created a milestone in getting their machine off the ground at Kitty Hawk, USA. Later in the World Wars of 1914-1918 and 1939-1945, flying developed at an astonishing rate when it was realised that wars could be won by air power. The development of rocket power by the Germans in the thirties made space travel a reality but because the Germans lost the war and their science leaders were poached by America and Russia, they never received due credit for their achievements in space technology.

With a book of this nature, it is difficult to know where to start. Volumes could be written about the inception and development of Hedon Aerodrome as a Municipal Airport from 1929 onwards. Mr E.F. (Ted) Winkler of Hedon has already researched and collected a considerable amount of material covering this period which may provide a background to more than one book. However, my purpose here is to commence from late 1956 when, effectively, my connection with the aerodrome began. Nevertheless, I do remember watching an Air Display there as a very small boy. This together with seeing the famous 'Graf Zeppelin' pass by in 1931 formed my earliest recollections of aviation. Shortly after this, my family moved from Patrington where I was born to Withernwick, a village near Hornsea and there the remainder of my boyhood was spent. My mother took up her post as headmistress of the village school and continued for more than thirty years until retiring in the early 1960s.

Some say that one's early years shape the entire pattern of subsequent life, a view which I tend to share. The indelible impressions of childhood and youth are made when the senses are at their keenest. Every experience is new with no foreknowledge against which to measure. Now, of course it is easy to look back on the mistakes of life with the benefit of hindsight but it is perhaps as well. Certainly, I regard my childhood years with the greatest nostalgia.

A quarter of the twentieth century had already elapsed before I was born on the 3rd December 1924. My earliest experiences were of the little cottage in Ings Lane, Patrington where I was born. This was the centre of my secure tiny world and seemingly so different from these troubled times. I suppose it is a marvellous illusion which is shared by all children with a settled home, insulated from the problems which come with adulthood. A bygone age: the 'twenties' which gradually drifted away in the 'thirties', finally to disappear forever in the crushing vortex of World War II. For me and I imagine most others, things were never quite the same again after the war, but more of that later.

What I was not immediately aware of in my first years was that I had been born into the traumatic era following the Great War of 1914-1918. The relative calm of the early 1900s which my parents had experienced was merely the lull before the storm. The catastrophic consequences of nearly a million dead and twice as many wounded or maimed must have been very apparent to the adults of the time. The flower of young manhood had been practically wiped out of that generation on the battlefields of Northern France – the Somme, Ypres Salient, Passchendaele. There were many young widows and spinsters who remained alone and isolated all their lives because around Vimy Ridge there were simply not enough young men left to balance.

The Second World War came in 1939, eventually taking me overseas and away from the area. I renewed my passion for flying in the early fifties and took a flying licence with Skegness Aero Club at Ingoldmells in Lincolnshire. With the phasing out of the flying club at Speeton, near Bridlington at this time, Skegness was in fact the nearest facility. Nearly all the keen young men from Hull flew at Skegness in the fifties and a number had learnt to fly through the ATC (Air Training Corps) and the CCF (Combined Cadet Force) Flying Scholarship Scheme.

Although it was relatively cheap to fly in those days, the travelling cost to and from Skegness, as well as the inconvenience of crossing the River Humber by ferryboat consumed both time and money. I decided to invest in a light aeroplane on the assumption that it would be easy to find somewhere to operate from on the Hull side of the river, therefore reducing costs. Unfortunately, this idea did not work out so my DH Tiger Moth remained in the Ingoldmells hangar thus increasing my flying budget.

In 1949, I qualified as a teacher at Saltley College, Birmingham but owing to a low salary and with a young family, I switched to commerce in the early fifties. My sponsored activities in athletics and rugby kept me fit and helped balance my life. My early recollection of Hedon was during a 1930 open day; I was sitting in the back of a Morris Oxford wearing what was termed a 'Dickie' hat. A twenty-six year gap from 1930 brought me to 1956 when I found myself waiting around the old aerodrome trying to assess its state for light aircraft flying. At the time I was looking for a suitable site in the Hull area from which to fly the old Tiger Moth which I had just acquired for £360.

But my chance came in 1956 and 1957 after receiving a favourable reply from the Hull Corporation regarding the usage of the former Municipal airport at Hedon. The seeds were sown in my mind to have a local airfield near Hull so that we could all fly from here. My Hedon Aerodrome reconnaissance in 1957 condensed my ideas.

Since then, the Hull Corporation has provided me with two channels on my account to have a local, close-in air terminal for the city. One of course, Hedon Aerodrome (1959-60), and ten years later, Paull Aerodrome, my own particular brain child built on virgin soil. These projects took the guts out of my life during my best years and both included supported failure. If there had been a successful outcome to my forty-five years ago projects, this account would not have been necessary.

Not long after the First World War ended in 1918, the idea of establishing a municipal airport for the city of Hull was being considered by some councillors. However, it was not until 1928 that the Hull Corporation agreed to search for a suitable site on which to establish an aerodrome. At that time, a few other forward thinking provincial city councils were doing likewise and the Government of the day gave encouragement for such ventures.

Under the guidance of the Director of Civil Aviation, Air Vice-Marshall Sir Sefton Brancker, and also the Air Minister Lord Thompson, civil aviation had made great advances at that time. Tragically, both men were to die shortly afterwards at Beauvais, Northern France in October 1930, when the Airship R101 came down whilst en route to India on her maiden flight.

The Air Navigation Act 1920 and the Public Work Facilities Act 1930 meant that suitable aerodrome sites could be acquired by compulsory purchase with the assistance of loans. From a number of other options, the Hull Corporation selected the old Hedon racecourse as being the best site. Hedon Racecourse was purchased by the Corporation in 1929 from the East Riding Club and Racecourse Company for £17,000. Incidentally, horseracing had taken place here from 1888 to 1909 but lack of support had forced its closure. At that time, the small Hedon halt platform was in operation to ferry passengers from Hull as had been the vogue for horserace meetings. The last race was on the 11 September 1909 when only four horses ran.

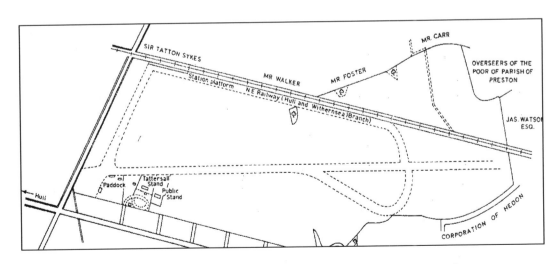

The Hedon Racecourse in 1913, taken from a plan in a sale catalogue now present in the Hull City Council Record Office.

On Saturday the 13 July 1912, seventeen years before the opening of Hedon Aerodrome, the very first flying demonstration in the Hull area was given by pilot Gustav Hamel. He made a number of flights from the old racecourse, occasionally taking passengers up as well. When Gustav landed his Bleriot monoplane on the site, local folk turned out to marvel at this new invention. The large crowds who gathered included the Lord Mayors of Hull and Hedon with other civic heads being present. Local reporters had commented on how Hamel had glided over the ground, with the 'crowds filled with doubt as to whether he would clear the rails. This fear was soon removed, for he quickly reached a height of about 500 feet and sailed away amid a storm of applause.' Hamel was already somewhat famous for being the first official flying postman, an accolade he gained after delivering over 100,000 letters and cards marking the coronation of HRH King George V in September 1911.

Previously unseen photograph of Gustav Hamel at Hedon in 1912

The outbreak of the First World War in July 1914 grounded any further civil flying, with the Hedon Racecourse site being used by the East Yorkshire Regiment as a garrison town and storage for heavy artillery. In 1915, Mr W.R. Watkinson chose the site as the 'collecting ground' for Holderness inhabitants leaving their villages in the event of an invasion by German forces. Between March and October 1916, the site was used as a night landing site fir the Royal Aircraft factory B.E.2 biplanes of the Royal Fighting Corps No. 33 Squadron.

Hedon Aerodrome was intended as a 'close-in' airport on the edge of the city for quick and easy access, as were all municipal airports at the time. There was also the possibility of a seaplane slipway being established at Paull on the riverside, only two miles away. The whole idea of airports close to centres of population seems to have been lost in modern times. The setting up of London City Airport on the East India docks only a few miles from the west end is a welcome return to basics of air communication. The technology for STOL (Short Take-off and Landing) aircraft has been around for many years but seems to have been obscured by the jumbo-jet mentality (i.e. Boeing Aircraft's world monopoly on big passenger jets) which has more to do with money than convenience.

The municipal airport was officially opened by HRH Prince George, Duke of Kent, on the 10 April 1929. The Duke reportedly said at the time that 'no city or town will be able to hold its own without adequate facilities for aircraft'. The aerodrome opening was accompanied by an air display and afterwards, the Duke flew back to London. He was in fact a qualified pilot and wore the much coveted RAF pilot's wings. Tragically, the Duke would be killed in a crash involving a Sunderland patrol aircraft in 1942, while in RAF service.

Hull was in fact the third city in the country to establish a municipal airport, just being short-headed by Manchester and Bristol. That same year, the Hull Flying Club was also founded and operated by National Flying Services. A spacious bungalow served both as an office and a clubhouse, and a hangar with ambulance station was erected on the western side of the landing area. Later, on the 11 August 1930, Hull rejoiced when local girl Amy Johnson returned home after her epic Australia flight, becoming the city's sweetheart overnight. The airfield was opened to the public for the momentous occasion. Hull had the best possible start for the launch of their airport but what happened afterwards looked disappointing, with golden opportunities being literally thrown away.

National Flying Services aimed to increase the interest in flying within the general public by staging several displays at the airfield. Sir Alan Cobham and his flying circus performed there for this very reason and even the 'flying flea' from France paid the town a visit. The erection of a nearby airport garage to allow the manufacture of light aircraft was a further attempt at attracting visitors and industry within the vicinity of the aerodrome.

During the thirties, perhaps the highpoint was on the 31 May 1934, when the inaugural flight from Holland to Hedon took place for the commencement of the KLM service. On board were the Lord Mayor of Hull (Alderman A. Shepherd), the Chairman of Hull Development Committee (Ald. F. Till), the Chairman of Hull Aerodrome (Ald. Benno Pearlman) and Mrs Pearlman. Mr Clifford North, Head of C.B. North Ltd., the Hedon Road timber firm, was also on the flight from Holland (Schiphol airport). The aircraft was a three-engine Fokker F12 high-wing monoplane, piloted by Captain Ivan Smirnoff – Chief Pilot of KLM who had commenced his flying career as a Russian fighter pilot in the First World War. He also held the world record in flying hours of 29,000 at that time. What a splendid send off this service had with 10,000 people turning out to watch proceedings.

Another route was prepared by Hillman Airways Limited in June 1935, connecting Hull with Manchester, Liverpool and Belfast, but the company folded the following year. Another short-lived venture was the 'Humber Air Ferry' using a twin-engine Blackburn Seagrave aircraft to fly between Hedon and Grimsby. All of this activity proved somewhat entertaining to the public, and for many people around the city of Hull, driving to the aerodrome on Sundays and watching the brightly coloured twin-engine planes take off and land proved to be the highlight of their week.

Fokker F.XII-3m or F.XII airliner – The inauguration of the KLM service from Amsterdam on 31 May 1934

Regrettably, KLM air services to Hedon were stopped in 1935 through lack of support. The British weather played somewhat of a part in this, but it had also become apparent that the city would require an airfield better equipped to allow for night-time and all-weather flying. Nevertheless, I wish that I could have been around at the time to keep the thing going and feel that much more needed to have been done to ensure adequate support. Obviously, the aerodrome committee were not doing their job. In my opinion, you need flying enthusiasts to handle airfield affairs, not accountants and committee men. Incidentally, several airline companies proposed operating from Hedon in 1935 and 1936, with services from Southampton and Nottingham and London and Aberdeen mentioned. North Eastern Airways had offered connections to Croydon, Grimsby, Doncaster and Manchester in 1937 but the following year they were halted.

On the 3 September 1939 in the clubhouse at Hedon, a group of club pilots and some RAF VR pilots listened with riveted attention to a radio broadcast on that Sunday morning at 11 am. It was of course the now famous declaration of war speech by the then Prime Minister, Sir Neville Chamberlain. Amongst the group of young pilots was the legendary 'Ginger' Lacey, who would become renowned as one of the top scoring RAF fighter pilots during the Second World War and the second highest scoring British RAF pilot of the Battle of Britain. Sadly, Jimmy Lacey passed on some years ago but I regard it as an honour to have been a Co-director of East Yorkshire Aero Co. Ltd. with him.

Flying continued without interruption for ten years up to the outbreak of World War Two on the 3 September 1939. The Air Navigation (restrictions in time of war) Order 1939 brought to an end all civil flying in the UK. In February 1940, civil aerodromes were requisitioned for war purposes, including Hedon. From a planning point of view, the war therefore prevented the existing use of the land for the duration of the emergency, and of course long after the war ended in 1945, owing to damage from wartime uses. Before the war, National Flying Services had used Hedon with an aim to host scheduled flights. Once war began the site was used to train glider pilots, although prior to this it had been surveyed as a possible military airfield but the proposal was rejected. The main reason was that it was considered to be too close to the oil tanks at the neighbouring Salt End works.

During the Second World War, there were perhaps a thousand military airfields operating on the British Isles; like a gigantic aircraft carrier floating off the European coast. Because of these and without any doubt, victory was finally achieved in 1945 by superior air power. Diverted from the spring board of our islands, it is all the more astonishing that therefore even in the late fifties, twelve years after the cessation of hostilities, Hull still did not have an air terminal serving the city. True, there had been some residual fear of aeroplanes by the City Fathers owing to heavy wartime bombing of the city.

Hull was one of the most heavily 'blitzed' cities during the war, suffering considerable damage and casualties. Its importance as a busy port made it a focal point of attacks by the German Luftwaffe from September 1939 until the last raid, on 17 March 1945. There were, in total, eighty-two raids on the city although this was never publicly revealed at the time, with the BBC referring to Hull as a 'north-east town' due to censorship rules. Around 1,200 people lost their lives and more than 3,000 were injured, but the bravery of the residents was rewarded by visits from Their Majesties King George VI and Queen Elizabeth, as well as Prime Minister Winston Churchill. The raids inevitably left the city in a very poor state financially.

As a fighting soldier in World War II, my main interests afterwards were aviation and sport. Of the Hull City councillors, few if any fought in the Second World War being too old or otherwise engaged. Likewise everyone, young and old, was sucked into the giant vacuum of WWII in some form or another. I was fourteen years old when war was declared.

The land around Hedon was protected by a safeguard plan, monitored by the Air Ministry to prevent excessive building development which would of course encroach on the aerodrome approaches. The Town and Country Planning Act of 1932 empowered local authorities to define 'zones' or areas within which the height of the buildings and other development could be regulated in the vicinity of the aerodromes. Excessive development could also be prevented or controlled. This carried on until at least July 1945 when buildings were restricted to a height of not more than 100 feet on Somerden Road, which became Priestman's Factory. This was almost ¾ mile from the Western boundary of the aerodrome. The plan is shown in a copy of the Kingston-upon-Hull (South-East Hull and District) Town Planning Scheme 1933. This scheme was in operation until the 1 July 1948, the date when the Town and Country Planning Act 1947 came into operation.

After being rejected by the RAF, the airfield became a dumping ground for hundreds of cars, the purpose being to render the landing of enemy aircraft impossible, should the event arise. This inevitably prevented the immediate resumption of the aerodrome after the war, due to the damage not being put to rights by the Air Ministry and the War Department. The Hull Corporation never did settle this matter so that my company had to make good the aerodrome after our go-ahead for flying in December 1958, before an aerodrome licence could be obtained.

In the immediate post-war period from May 1945, it was clear that Hedon Aerodrome was unusable for flying purposes because of the legacy of wartime earthworks, gun emplacements and WD huts. Immediately after the war, in October 1946, a demonstration was given at the airfield using a German Dornier

211

aircraft by a Nottingham firm. The event, witnessed by the Hull Corporation Town Planning Committee, saw the plane take off, fly around and then land. During this, the plane rather unfortunately hit a pothole damaging the aircraft's undercarriage.

Between 1947 and 1949, around twelve acres of the site were used by the 'Hull's Angels' as a speedway motorcycle track. Despite the clubhouse being renovated and the hangar being used as a grandstand, the venture proved unsuccessful. Later on, twenty acres of the site were let to the East Riding TA Association and a piece was sold to the Distiller's Company (then titled British Industrial Solvents) for use as playing fields. The remainder, however, was still reserved for flying. Minutes of the aerodrome committee up to the committee standing down on the 11 July 1951 make for uninspiring reading. After standing down, the Town Planning Committee then took over responsibility for the site.

A motorcyclist using the old Hedon speedway track – 1950s

In January 1957, I contacted Town Planning requesting flying use of the Aerodrome. The 'go-ahead' to fly was given in December 1958. No effort seemed to have been made to tidy up the airfield and get some flying underway again. In fairness to the Town Planning Committee who took over responsibility in 1951, they did at least respond to my request to fly there.

Hedon Aerodrome as seen from over the River Humber, with King George Dock in the Foreground and the Oil Storage Tanks at Saltend to the right – 1938

It is said that Historians, Politicians and some others are granted a talent that even the Gods are denied, that is 'to alter what has already happened'. I quote the following:

1.　　In a 'Hull Daily Mail' report of 8th October 1979, it stated that 'war spelt the end of flying at Hedon, apart from an unsuccessful attempt in the early 1960s to promote a businessmen's air service to London'.

2.   A private and confidential report issued in 1961 by the Hull Corporation Town Planning Department and entitled 'A civil airport for Kingston upon Hull' did not become available to the public until 1991, under the 30-year rule. In the section headed 'Hedon Aerodrome 1929-1960', number 13 states that 'the use of Hedon Aerodrome was suspended during the war and flying has not been resumed since'.

3.   In the Hull Chamber of Commerce Annual Report of 1962-1963 and under a section headed 'Local Air Service Facilities' (page 28, line 14) it states 'this maintained pressure has taken the form of repeated approaches to the Hull Corporation regarding the possible greater use of the former Hedon Aerodrome, the feeling being that a substantial proportion of the local demand would be met if more regular and adequate arrangements could be made for small executive type aircraft to use that site. Aircraft of this kind require but little in the way of landing ground facilities and the more ready availability of the Hedon airfield for the use of these aircraft would be of considerable benefit, a statement borne out by the increasing frequency with which certain companies have made use of the facility notwithstanding that the procedure involved is evidently subject on occasion to some delay'.

2.

The True Facts

My own direct experiences of Hedon Aerodrome began on a cold, foggy autumn day in 1956; I tramped around the pre-war Hull municipal airport near Hedon. My search for a light aircraft terminal near Hull went no further, thus a decision was made there and then. Here was the obvious place. True, there was a substantial amount of old wartime debris littered almost everywhere with concrete and trenches from military uses. All this would have to be cleared, but there was still enough room for take-off and landing in some parts. The hangar was in good condition, with toilets, and a hut nearby was suitable for a clubhouse.

After brief research, I contacted the Hull Corporation who owned the land, requesting permission to fly from the aerodrome. This was in January 1957. Following almost two years of protracted negotiations, the Corporation gave the go-ahead to fly on the 1 December 1958.

A very enthusiastic group of local young people were impatient to get started and this showed promise for a great future, or so it was thought. Two years later, I and my colleagues were told to vacate the premises. It is incredible that one is finished almost before starting – and this book is the story of what happened during those incredible years.

From the beginning, this project was embarked upon with trust, out in the open with nothing hidden. Just about everyone knew about our plans including the heads of industry. There were many supporters and Col J.B. Upton, then Chairman of Reckitts, had already decided to become a member of the new flying club, having been Chairman of the pre-war Hull Aero Club.

However, and unknown to me at that time, there were others who were conspiring with a cunningly orchestrated plan to prevent the development of flying at Hedon Aerodrome. Our 'go-ahead' for flying on an 'existing use right' was ignored by the East Riding County Council and an objection to our flying by the Distillers Company at Saltend caused the County Council to turn down planning. They were of course all in league with each other having had two and a half years notice of impending flying, but choosing to ignore it until the plot had thickened in their favour.

From my side, the project was embarked upon with trust, out in the open, with nothing hidden. I wish that the same could be said of those with ulterior motives, who were opposed to it. The readers may draw their own conclusions as the story unfolds.

Now, after more than forty years, I can only feel very cynical about the grossly over-developed Saltend industrial complex, with the threat of yet more to come. I am prompted to say 'I told you so' for in my opinion, light aviation at Hedon Aerodrome would have kept the greenbelt green. The industries and authorities have a lot to answer for – they collectively prevented the expansion of light aviation in the Hull area from the fifties to the present day. At a personal level, it certainly kept me out of a career in civil aviation.

Perhaps my disgust may best be summarised by reference to my original rallying point – De Havilland 'Tiger Moth' aeroplane registration G-ANEJ. After eviction from Hedon in 1961, the poor old aeroplane moved through half a dozen temporary homes before ending up in the Malaysian Air Force Museum in Kuala Lumpur (1989). No words can describe my disgust over the reasons or the people who caused all this to happen. I wish Hull's famous Amy Johnson was still around to comment!

Prior to the formation of the East Yorkshire Aero Company, I had campaigned as an individual for the use of Hedon airfield, the pre-war municipal airport of Hull and owned by the Hull Corporation. This airfield had been out of use more or less since the 1939-45 war but I managed to persuade the Hull Corporation to allow the use of a portion of the old airfield, mainly as a flying club. It was for this reason that my company was incorporated as the East Yorkshire Aero Club

Ltd. on the 8 May 1959, the title considered to be appropriate at that time. In 1964, this title was changed because the word 'club' in aviation creates an adverse impression and is regarded as something small and rather amateurish.

A letter was posted on the 7 January 1957 to the Corporation and a follow up letter ten days later. In the meantime, the Corporation replied with speedy acknowledgement, the matter being subsequently raised at a full Town Planning Committee meeting on the 24 January 1957 and again at a sub-committee meeting on the 31 January 1957.

The overall result was that an encouraging letter arrived from the Town Clerk; Mr Ernest H. Bullock, the content of which I considered to be very favourably disposed towards flying from Hedon again. The Corporation themselves were quite adamant about not wishing to have any financial commitment on flying activities so the ball was very much in my court. Clearly, without financial assistance, it would take some time to organise suitable proposals which might be acceptable to the Corporation.

After a further exchange of correspondence during mid-1957, another year was to drag by before the project could be condensed. I had no capital with which to float a company, so it was a question of gathering together a group of colleagues to share the load. By 1958, a number of issues had to be sorted out, not least was to plan out a flying area from the existing 200 acres of land. An official aerodrome licence was required from the Ministry of Civil Aviation as it was then known. In those days, the northern division of the Ministry was based in Liverpool and the officials were former World War II fliers almost to a man. They most certainly knew what they were talking about.

From the outset, Clive Hullock dealt with the Hedon issue. He was a fine man who had been a chief flying instructor during the war and whose responsibility had been to train considerable numbers of embryo Royal Air Force pilots. Later, Mr Hullock was to give supporting evidence both on our behalf and the Hull Corporation, at the three day public inquiry of February 1960.

My liaisons with the Ministry commenced in late 1957 and Mr Hullock first visited Hedon Aerodrome on the 7 August 1958. Initial discussions were to agree a suitable minimum flying area for club type aircraft which could be licensed as an aerodrome. This piece of land had to come from an area at the western end between two substantial barbed wire fences running north to south across the field, enclosing about 100 acres. Front line soldiers would have welcomed such protection but for aircraft, the wire represented yet another hurdle or hazard to flying, with the grazing cattle always taking precedent over everything else. Readers may draw their own conclusions as to why this should be.

Eventually an area of about 57 acres was agreed with the MTCA as being adequate to obtain an aerodrome licence for club aircraft. The Town Planning Department passed the details on to the Treasurer's Department for action over rental charges and a draft lease.

Mr Jack Allan dealt with these negotiations on behalf of the City Treasurer. He was a pleasant, diplomatic man who had to somehow work out agreement between ourselves and Mr Stamford Smith, the farmer who then held the grazing rights on most of Hedon Aerodrome. Unfortunately for us, Mr Smith was intransigent on the flying issue and disliked aeroplanes. The purpose of the wire fences being to contain grazing cattle owned by the tenant farmer.

My first inkling of third party interest came in the late summer of 1958, when Mr Allan asked whether it was possible to make a slight modification in the SW corner of our 57-acre plan at the request of the Distillers Company at Saltend. Unknown to me, DCL had managed to obtain a 99-year lease on a number of acres there for a sports field and then my assumption was that they must have sewn the deal up before my flying request. Not so. A few years later, the minutes of the Town Planning Committee revealed that my flying request (Resolution 11307) preceded British Industrial Solvents sports field inquiry (Resolution 11589) by some months. Just who was pulling the strings or what sort of game the Corporation were playing, I had no idea.

At that time, I did not regard the sports field as critical to flying and there did not appear to be any ulterior motives. At any rate, our impending flying was known about. The simple modification was approved by the MTCA and the relevant plans were illustrated. It seemed a trifling matter and presented no problem at the time but in the light of subsequent events, proved to be a key overall issue. The simple modification was approved by the MTCA without fuss.

The local Territorial Army Association held a lease on several acres of land at the western end of the aerodrome, which included the hangar but they were not using it at that time. Thankfully, an associate made a very kind gesture in allowing the embryo East Yorkshire Aero Club to use it. I suppose that my membership of the T.A. may have helped.

By late summer of 1958, agreement with the MTCA, T.A. and provisional association with the Hull Corporation had been obtained. The latter were influenced by my letter dated the 9 August 1958 in which I gave the names of pilots and student pilots who had guaranteed support for the club. Resolution 13284 of the Town Planning Committee minutes, which were passed at their August 1958 meeting, indicates provisional approval as does the Town Planning Officer's letter dated the 20 August 1958.

The controlling body of flying clubs, The Association of British Aero Clubs based in London, had already received our application for affiliation as the 'EAST YORKSHIRE AERO CLUB' and this was being processed. A draft lease was being prepared by Mr Peter Bilton, a solicitor who acted for us and liaised with the City Treasurer throughout. At the same time, Michael Heathcote as financial advisor was in charge of money matters. Both were to become Directors of the club in 1959 when a limited company was formed.

By September 1958, everything was at last coming together. Provisional agreement had now been made with all interested parties including the Hull Corporation, the MTCA, the T.A. Association and to some extent with Mr Smith over the grazing rights. A considerable amount of background work had to be undertaken during the last months of 1958 on the administrative side. However, it all seemed worthwhile because the culmination of our efforts was reached in the shape of a letter received from Mr C.H. Pollard, the City Treasurer, dated the 1 December, 1958.

Here at last was the long awaited 'go-ahead' from the Hull Corporation. It was pure magic to us. The real hard practical work on the ground had yet to begin but none of our young enthusiastic supporters minded that. Not a cloud in the sky could be seen and it was inconceivable to us that anything could possibly go wrong now.

During the winter of '58-'59, occasional excursions across the River Humber were made to Ingoldmells Airfield, near Skegness for a spot of flying, as my Tiger Moth G-ANEJ was still hangared there. It was a long way to go for flying, but it was going to be some months before the aeroplane could be based at Hedon.

To kick off the New Year of 1959, a combined club circular and application form was prepared, copies of which were sent out from the 20 January onwards. Our mailing list included a number of pre-war Hull Aero Club fliers and the response was excellent. This dispelled any lingering doubts which I might have had for future success. Even Colonel J.B. Upton, at that time Chairman of Reckitt and Colman, sent an affirmative reply. As well as being a notable pre-war pilot, he had been Chairman of the original Hull Aero Club.

One of the first practical jobs to do on the aerodrome was to bulldoze a taxiway gap through the speedway spectator banking in order to gain access to the flying field. This banking of about ten feet consisted of 'Blitz' bombing rubble from the city deposited there just after the war. It is still there. In February 1959, a bulldozer was duly hired from Cook's 'airport garage' on the south side of the Aerodrome, the rubble clearance taking about two days. The garage with original motif still stands there as a constant reminder that here was the Hull municipal airport of the thirties.

On the 8 February 1959, my great friend the late Ken Charles came with me from Skegness in the Tiger to touch down for the first time at Hedon. It was a pity that we had to return to Ingoldmells but there was far too much ground work to be done at home.

We had already established ourselves on the site in a derelict but serviceable War Department hut next to the hangar. The original pre-war clubhouse, a large imposing wooden building had unfortunately been sold by a department of the Hull Corporation to the department handling the Sutton Park Golf Club just after the war. I consider this to have been a hasty and ill-conceived deal when most of the RAF fliers of the war were still in the service, who would form the backbone of a flying club when demobbed.

The hangar itself was in a mess, having been used as a 'foldyard' by Mr Smith for his cattle. His less than a year tenancy agreement with the Corporation for grazing rights did not include the use of the hangar as the Territorial Army Association held the lease on this land. It was grossly out of order but we had to clear the mess before the hangar could be used for aircraft. There was at least two feet of manure on the floor and backrooms covering an area of 90 feet by 60 feet. It took weeks to clear and hose down to get rid of the smell. Even the backroom of the hangar had not escaped the attention of the cattle and I considered this to be a flagrant abuse on the part of the farmer of a building. Ironically, it was as clean as a new pin when I first inspected the site more than two years before. Needless to say, we had to clean it out ourselves.

Work continued on the hut for use as a clubhouse and bar. The latter stage was never reached. Electricity and water were laid on as an early priority and Don Askem managed to connect the hangar lights.

As the weather improved with the arrival of spring, a close inspection of the aerodrome surface revealed that much more work was necessary than originally thought for the safe take-off and landing of aircraft. It should not really have been our responsibility. Although the war had ended fourteen years before, the Hull Corporation had never sorted out the outstanding war damage claims. The aerodrome had never been reinstated to its pre-war condition after various wartime uses and requisitions by the Air Ministry War Department. It certainly should have been done years before and paid for by the Governmental departments concerned. A wide variety of wartime uses other than aviation had heavily damaged and also left the surface in a poor state. One thing was for sure, no one was going to pay our little group for extensive site clearance. Furthermore we would have to pay rent on the land for flying purposes when it could not be used as such, until cleared.

The Corporation had made a great shout regarding the grazing in the 'go-ahead' letter of December 1958, to quote: 'If the land is to be kept in good order and prevent the growth of weeds which would have an adverse effect on the value of the land for future grazing.' With hindsight, there was nothing right about this and other statements. What an astonishing attitude towards an operational aerodrome! I would doubt very much whether the City Fathers had ever set foot on Hedon anyway.

In fact, the grass, weeds and all had overgrown the rubbish and rubble left from the war on parts of the aerodrome. These were the problems that we had to face and tackle but at that time, the small print of the December letter passed unobserved, so happy were we to get started. Tractors and trailers were loaned for rubble clearance at weekends.

The rubble was deposited in the north-west corner of the aerodrome and grew into a large heap by late summer 1959, running into many tonnes. Quite a number of concrete pillars strewn across the airfield were also removed. These had been erected as possible German glider obstruction in case of invasion early in the war. Fortunately for the aero club, the tractors and trailers were loaned 'gratis' from Robert Holtby, a farmer and personal friend of Skirlaugh, and John Dimishky of Preston, to whom we were much indebted.

Working parties with members allotted various tasks continued throughout the summer to render the aerodrome suitable for the issue of an aerodrome licence from the Ministry of Civil Aviation. There was a strict set of criteria to meet. About the same time, contact was made with the Army Royal Engineers, a Territorial Army unit based at Sutton. They had access to some very good equipment and confirmed that they could level the ground at Hedon, where necessary. This would be done as weekend exercises.

A landmark in our progress was the erection of a pole on which to attach a windsock obtained from British Petroleum at Saltend, with BP insignia displayed. Our aviation petrol was obtained from this source. The windsock was just about the best advertisement of flying activities taking place.

Everything seemed to be going very nicely. Our lease with the Hull Corporation was ready but suddenly and out of the blue came an unexpected setback.

In those days, the Hull-Withernsea railway branch line still operated, although it was to close in 1964 under the Doctor Beeching plan. The line ran along the northern boundary of the aerodrome.

3.

Trouble Beckons

Around mid-April 1959, it was noticed that a working gang had commenced to erect a row of telegraph poles along the railway side where none had previously existed. This of course represented a substantial hazard to aircraft taking off and landing in that direction. Furthermore, the flying area of 57 acres on which the lease was based and vetted by the Civil Aviation Ministry for the issue of an aerodrome licence was thrown into jeopardy.

On enquiry, I was informed by the work foreman that British Railways had decided in their wisdom to replace the previously buried underground cables with overhead wires on poles. Incredible though it may seem, the foreman and gang already knew all about the re-opening of Hedon for flying but carried on regardless under orders. The original cables had been laid underground in 1934, precisely to maintain an unrestricted flying approach from the north, in the old municipal airport days of the thirties. I have always felt that the timing of this episode by British railways was quite deliberate. With the full knowledge of flying and no prior consultation with Hull Corporation or the Aero Club, they had created a new, additional hazard.

Mr Ian McGregor, the senior BR Executive in Hull, was contacted immediately and requested to urgently deal with this matter. Mr Alston, the Chief Town Planning Officer of Hull was also prevailed upon. In a very short time, every relevant department of Hull Corporation knew about the poles, whilst in the meantime, British Rail had spirited the problem away to their headquarters at York. There, safely in the hands of a General Manager at BR's North-Eastern region, nothing was ever going to be done to shift the pole hazard. It simply got lost in the hierarchy.

The next thing was for Clive Hullock of the Civil Aviation Ministry to pick up the pieces of our carefully planned and agreed flying area of 1958, on which the lease was based. The continued presence of the poles imposed a permanent operational restriction which was to drag on into 1960, without ever being settled.

At about the same time, a surveyor for the Holderness Rural District Council, Mr H.L. Ingham called round to inspect a temporary petrol store in the back of the hangar. Unfortunately, the pre-war underground fuel tanks had been rendered unusable at the beginning of the war.

Mr Ingham casually enquired whether planning permission had been applied for to fly at Hedon. I replied that the 'go-ahead' had been given by the Corporation in December 1958. The matter was duly passed on to my solicitor, Mr Peter Bilton, who took it up with East Riding County Council for clarification.

Flying preparations were now sufficiently advanced to transfer the Tiger Moth aircraft from Skegness to Hedon. This particular milestone took place on Friday, 15 May 1959 when I flew across the Humber with Ken Charles to land at Hedon in the evening. It was dull with low cloud down to 500 feet. We did get some press coverage, thus the whole district would now be aware of flying at Hedon, even if earlier publicity in 1958 and Corporation committee minutes from 1957 had been missed.

Tiger Moth dropped in on Hedon

A PLANE LANDED AT HEDON AIRFIELD last night—and that surprised the inhabitants. For the airfield now is strictly for the cows. They were so surprised that one man telephoned Hedon police, who sent a sergeant and a constable to see what it was all about.

The explanation was quite simple.

The plane—a little Tiger Moth—belongs to the newly-formed East Yorkshire Aero Club, Ltd.

MANAGING DIRECTOR

They had leased a portion of the old landing ground from Hull Corporation, and the plane was the first of several they plan to buy for their members.

The managing director, 32-year-old Mr Neville Medforth, who works for a Hull rivercraft firm, went down to Skegness to take delivery of the silver two-seater aircraft, and with RAF National Serviceman Ken Charles, of 63, Cranswick-gr., Hull, as passenger, flew it up to Hedon. Charles, who is on leave, is a qualified pilot.

They touched down at 8.30 as the light was failing.

"We had to keep low all the way because of low cloud," Mr Medforth explained.

SAFELY LOCKED UP

Now G-ANEJ is safely chocked up and locked up in the airfield's small hanger—and Hedon should soon be accustomed to seeing planes circling their airfield once more.

Tiger Moth dropped in on Hedon: Hull Daily Mail, 16 May 1959

Regarding the Holderness Rural District Council planning query, the Hull Corporation was surprisingly reticent, merely suggesting that we should carry on flying. Surely, the Town Planning Department of a city with 300,000 inhabitants must have cleared the planning issues more than two years before, as far back as January 1957. The flying 'go-ahead' of the 1 December 1958 meant exactly what it said.

With the aeroplane now at Hedon, flying was a daily occurrence which was of course the whole purpose of being there. During the next few months, substantial numbers of visitors came down to either watch, enquire or hopefully fly. With only one home based aircraft available, flights were restricted to club members and their friends but there were some visiting aircraft coming on. Another attraction at that time was army parachute training from static balloons by the Army reserve unit, the 299 Parachute Squadron Royal Engineers and I remember with great nostalgia making several parachute drops onto the aerodrome.

Taken around June 1959 – 299 Parachute Field Squadron RE – Weekend drop at Hedon

But storm clouds were gathering over the East Riding County Council's insistence on planning approval. Although Hull Corporation owned Hedon Aerodrome (and still do), the airfield lay just outside the Hull city boundary and came within Holderness RDC jurisdiction, as part of ERCC. Under Labour Government post-war legislation, the Town and Country Act of 1947 was introduced, with rigid draconian planning rules. Before World War Two, such restrictions did not exist.

Peter Bilton requested a formal determination on the planning issue from ERCC on the basis of the aerodrome having an 'existing use right' under the Planning Act of 1947, which did not require planning approvals. Nevertheless, the ERCC were adamant about the need to submit a planning application. With hindsight of course they would, wouldn't they, as a trap was being set by them.

With the Corporation sitting on the fence, the club was in a quandary. Distillers Company at Saltend were threatening injunctions if flying continued, as a danger to their factory. The fact that DCL had known of our flying plans from the very beginning in January 1957 and had not objected then was all the more disturbing.

Strangely, it still had not occurred to me that a cunningly orchestrated plot had been devised to prevent flying and, stage by stage, was being implemented. My total commitment to the aerodrome project had prevented me from spotting the blatant official deceit. My reasoning hinged on the Corporation 'go-ahead' of 1958 and not a whisper about planning in the previous two years. So why then should there be a crisis?

Although the Hull Town Planning Officer Mr Alston had said 'carry on', my late father who was Chairman of our little company at that time, liked to have things right, so a planning application was submitted to Holderness RDC on the 10 September 1959. Needless to say, a reply came in double quick time. The letter dated the 23 September from Holderness RDC, rejecting planning, was accompanied by a copy of a letter from DCL with a strong objection. So there it was. The trap had sprung and the East Yorkshire Aero Club was stuck in it. Following urgent discussions with the Corporation, we decided to appeal against the planning decision.

Flying had come to a shuddering halt and the project was put on ice to await the outcome of an impending appeal hearing. The Corporation authorities were saying 'leave the appeal to us'. In the event, I wished that I had conducted my own appeal as I knew far more about the aerodrome situation.

Canvassing for support in the Saltend area, we found that neither Shell, BP nor Esso objected to our flying nor did the East Riding fire chief who was responsible for fire safety in the Saltend area. This was re-assuring to us after DCL had made such a fuss about fire risk. All that remained was the question of waiting, somewhat impatiently, for an appeal hearing date; the weeks dragged by as autumn 1959 turned into winter. New Year 1960 arrived and still nothing. Three years had gone by since the original inquiry to Hull Corporation, which was simply outrageous.

Finally, after five months waiting and with practically no notice, a hearing date was fixed for the 10 February 1960. In addition, the whole issue had escalated into a public inquiry at the Guildhall in Hull, which was to last three days. The battle lines were drawn with the Hull Corporation and the Ministry of Civil Aviation on our side and the ERCC and DCL in opposition. In effect, the East Yorkshire Aero Club was stuck in 'no man's land' well and truly. The reasons for ERCC's planning refusal only arrived days before the inquiry date, giving quite inadequate time to mount a proper defence against their statements.

Senior Planning Officers and Barristers were aligned against each other, with the arbitrator, Mr A.R. Chown of the Ministry of Housing and Local Government, in the chair. The club had engaged a Hull barrister, Mr S.G. Davies, to represent us. It was all very confusing and a far cry from the flying project, like a nightmare come true in fact.

Maybe we were complacent; certainly the thought of losing the appeal never entered my head, with the might of Hull Corporation and the Civil Aviation Ministry in support. I felt sure that everything would be alright. However, when the inquiry got underway on Wednesday, 10 February 1960 in the Guildhall, my suspicions about an orchestrated plot against our flying were confirmed. The distortion and ignoring of fact was clearly evident and the atmosphere resembled an inquest.

The arbitrator acting on behalf of the Ministry of Housing and Local Government was a Mr Chown. Unfortunately, he had no concept of aviation or the local Hull scene where, for example, Mr Williamson the East Riding Chief Planning Officer referring to Hedon Aerodrome as Hedon racecourse, left a false impression. The racecourse had been closed in 1909, more than fifty years before the 1960 inquiry. A public inquiry is not a court of law as adverse planning decisions can be taken to the high court, but the costs involved in such things are astronomical and can ruin appellants. Forty years ago, it was almost impossible to reverse planning decisions, but nowadays, with ombudsmen it is easier and compensation may be claimed.

FLYING ACCIDENT COULD CAUSE SALTEND 'HOLOCAUST'

—INQUIRY TOLD

THE BRITISH TRANSPORT COMMISSION opposed the use of Hedon airfield for flying because whatever restrictions might be imposed to safeguard the Saltend petroleum installations any infringement might lead to an accident which might, without exaggeration, become a "holocaust involving heavy loss of life," said Mr Henry Littlefair, BTC surveyor, at the Hedon airfield inquiry at Hull Guildhall yesterday. The inquiry arises out of the refusal by East Riding County Council to grant the recently-formed East Yorkshire Aero Club, Ltd., permission to fly from Hedon airfield.

Mr Littlefair said that in 1958 about 2,000,000 tons of petroleum were processed at Saltend.

Mr John Howlett, general manager of the Distillers Company, Ltd., said that the premises were insured against fire for over £21,000,000.

QUITE A POINT

AT THE Hedon airfield inquiry at Hull Guildhall, Mr R. Holliday, Hull Corporation solicitor, rose to cross-examine Mr J. Williamson, East Riding County Planning Officer.

Many of their products were highly inflammable and dangerous. As much as 150,000 tons were produced each year and stocks held at the factory in tanks and drums exceeds 5,000,000 gallons.

"QUITE DREADFUL"

"The consequence of an aircraft accident within the factory, or at the neighbouring installations, which might elsewhere be negligible, could well be a devastating outbreak of fire and explosion," he said.

Mr J. F. S. Cobb, for the company, said that it would be "quite dreadful" if an aeroplane crashed into the premises. The loss of life would be "appalling."

He said Hull Corporation were using the aero club's application as "the thin end of the wedge" to open Hedon airfield to commercial flying.

"Sooner or later there would bound to be an accident," he said.

"Any damage to the company would be damage to the nation, because they are such vast exporters."

The inquiry closed.

Flying Accident Could Cause Saltend 'Holocaust' – Hull Daily Mail, 12 February 1960.

In 1930 and for a while afterwards light aircraft were constructed in the airport garage buildings on the south boundary of the airfield. Who could possibly have believed that some of the very industries originally encouraged to set up near Hedon, would eventually object to the airfield being there and attempt to force its closure.

In March 1962, I had hoped to stage a flying demonstration from the aerodrome in support, but I was not able to obtain the consent of Mr Smith to hold it. The reasons given were not financial (cash was offered) but he said that there would be some lambs and sheep on the airfield which he did not wish to be disturbed. However, the airfield remained deserted and had been for two months until that point. I was extremely annoyed by his attitude and felt that this must have been a deliberate excuse to prevent the demonstration being held, especially as the refusal had come only one week before.

Had the demonstration proceeded, there was to have been Ministry of Aviation representation, and apart from the twenty or so business and executive aircraft expected, I was hoping to have a 16/18 passenger Twin-Pioneer STOL (short take-off and landing) aircraft over from British United Airways. The manufacturers of the aircraft, Scottish Aviation of Prestwick, were keen to attend and found no problems landing at Hedon.

4.

Taking Stock

In the 1963 Annual Report of the Hull Chamber of Commerce and Shipping, there is a passage concerning local air service facilities. Within this, Hedon Aerodrome is discussed.

From my own observations, press reports of the time were in similar vein, but to actually read this in a representative annual report of the city was something of an insult. It was even worse reading down the council members list. The Senior Vice-President in 1963 was Mr John Howlett, General Manager of the Distillers Company at Saltend, the very company whose objection had forced me out of the aerodrome at the end of 1960.

The fact that I knew many of the council members personally did nothing for my confidence or credibility. Furthermore, several council members were provisional members of my East Yorkshire Aero Club in 1959, notably Col J.B. Upton, Chairman of Reckitt and Colman. I also had an interview with Mr Howlett in 1962 in an effort to reverse the DCL objection. There is a stigma attached to flying clubs by some, that club flying is more dangerous than, say, commercial flights. Nevertheless, most or all provincial airports have, in fact, flying schools operating, including Kirmington Airport.

In my opinion, the truth is that club flying being dangerous is only used as an excuse by those opposed to it. The pre-war municipal airport at Hedon was operated by Hull Aero Club (1934) Ltd. from that year on to the outbreak of war in September 1939. I think that the real reason why DCL wanted us out was to do with their own expansion plans, in other words – power, facilities or money talking.

Although our flying enquiry from Hedon in January 1957 preceded the DCL sports ground enquiry of April 1957, the Hull Corporation foolishly let this go through without a squeak whilst we were still negotiating for our lease and 'go-ahead' in December 1958. One thing is for sure, that DCL knew all about our flying plans from early 1957, yet did not object until September 1959 when our extensive preparations were almost complete. Unacceptable behaviour by a major company is a gross understatement and the indifference of the Hull Corporation cannot be condoned either.

Ironically in 1966, DCL was bought out by British Petroleum who had not objected to our flying prior to the February 1960 public inquiry. Somehow, looked at retrospectively, all these coincidences seem far from accidental.

Within a short time of my eviction from Hedon, backdoor flying commenced with executive business aircraft operated by or for large companies. Even in 1959, during my tenure, Harry Booth, an agent for Fenners, commuted regularly into Hedon by air. Without our cleaning-up operations of 1959, no aircraft would have been able to fly into Hedon then or later on.

To cut a long story short, the East Riding County Council moved in with Holderness District Council and an objection came from Distillers Company at Saltend ending in a three day public inquiry at the Guildhall in Hull on 10th, 11th and 12th February 1960. The negative result of my company's appeal did not come from the Ministry until early November 1960. The Hull Corporation would not take the matter to the High Court and my company lacked the financial resources to do so.

Thus after five years of negotiation, work and money spent, my company was back to square one. No compensation for loss was ever received from the corporation and the question of 'existing use right' and formal determination of planning was never settled. As far as I am concerned, Hedon was and still is an aerodrome and the Hull Corporation has never pursued the matter to continue flying on what could now have been a busy and useful air terminal for light aircraft.

Again, to cut a long story short, the Hull Corporation gave the go-ahead to use Hedon in December 1958 and a draft lease was drawn up. Unfortunately, this lease was never signed because an objection by an industrial concern nearby, the Distillers Company at Saltend, was upheld on appeal. My appeal on the refusal was supported by the Hull Corporation and the Ministry of Civil Aviation, but whilst a High Court appeal was considered, the corporation would not support this and my company had thus reluctantly to abandon the idea through lack of funds.

So it will be seen that within six months of its formation, the East Yorkshire Aero Co. was involved in an unsuccessful appeal, sandwiched in no man's land between two local authorities (Hull Corporation and East Riding County Council) battling it out over a piece of land with a Ministry and a public company thrown in for good measure. The position was hopeless, capital having been lost on preliminary preparations at Hedon and appeal legal costs with no redress. Another site had therefore to be found.

Returning to the appeal, the hearing report is quoted in full as issued by the Government inspector, Mr A.R. Chown, M.A., and A.M.T.P.I., Dip. T.P., including the result letter, dated 28 October 1960. Thus, the appeal result had taken about nine months after the original hearing. I consider this to be an absolute scandal especially as repeated requests had been made to the Ministry of Housing and Local Government for a decision. The result letter was a joke. A child could have written a better one and it looked as if the letter had been written by the inspector immediately after the hearing had finished, then been sat on for nine months before being sent. I cannot deny that I was flabbergasted.

The whole of our evidence and that of the Hull Corporation appeared to have been ignored including supporting evidence from the Ministry of Civil Aviation. Even the planning law itself relating to an 'existing use right' on Hedon Aerodrome had been ignored, namely sections 12 and 17 of the Town and Country Planning Act 1947 (effective from 1st July 1948). A planning decision is arbitration and an adverse decision can be taken to a High Court, that is to say, if you can afford it. In November 1960, I approached the Hull Corporation in an effort to persuade them to go to the High Court. The cost to them would have been peanuts. However, I could not move them. By now, two years had gone by since the 'go-ahead' of December 1958. The situation was outrageous.

My next move was to approach the association of British Aero Clubs and Centres in London. The head man there was a Group Captain G.H. Miles who was reputed to have influence in high circles. Eventually, a meeting was arranged to take place in London between representatives of the Ministry of Civil Aviation, the Ministry of Housing and Local Government, Group Capt. Miles and myself. Here was a possible ray of hope. Tragically, a few days before the arranged meeting, Captain Miles had a heart attack and died within a short time, thus I had to face the Ministry of my own. I did my best but lacked the 'clout' necessary to make enough impression. In 1961, I was told to vacate the premises. By 1962-1963, business aircraft users had started to fly in at Hedon by the 'back door'.

5.

Hedon today, Paull tomorrow

By virtue of the intransigence of the Hull Corporation to persist with the Hedon issue in the 1960-1965 period, I decided on behalf of my company to seek an alternative site to Hedon but still as near to the city as was available at that time. Some land became a possibility at Oxgoddes Farm, Paull, about eight miles from Hull city centre. After several years of fruitless searching, a suitable site was found between the villages of Paull and Thorngumbald in the East Riding, near Hull. From the airfield point of view, this was a virgin site being farmland near the River Humber.

It was decided to apply for planning approvals in April 1966, and only five years temporary planning was obtained in December 1966. This was of course totally inadequate commercially, but it was decided to press on in the hope that having got started, further planning could then be obtained. Planning approvals covered 145 acres, but initially only 65 acres were laid out as open ditches had to be culverted in order to obtain a suitable runway layout. This is quite costly and for a small £100 company with very limited capital, it was enough to commence with.

A lease was negotiated in 1967 with R.N. Leckonby and Sons, the landowners, and signed in February 1968. Although inadequate due to restricted planning and insufficient agreement with the landowners, again the company pressed on. This might be better understood within the context of the passage of nine years from the original formation of the company without any options having been fulfilled and no trading having taken place. I was naturally anxious to get started.

My company could not afford to buy the land so rental was the only other option. Temporary planning for five years was obtained in December 1966 but how the planning authority expected a company to develop an operational airfield on such terms I do not know. Paull was a virgin farmland site with open fields and ditches, and culverting and levelling was required before any idea of flying could be considered.

With the assistance of enthusiastic young men, as was the case at Hedon, the above work was carried out in a relatively short time but not without cost. By late 1968, an aerodrome licence was issued by the Ministry of Civil Aviation, and fairly soon, flying instruction commenced with the newly formed Hull Aero Club. Also, Bristow Helicopters, who served the North Sea oil rigs for BP, were desperate to find an alternative site having received notice from a temporary site at Tetney Lock, North Lincs. My company arrangements over their sub-tenancy were unsatisfactory from the start. At that time, Bristow Helicopters was the largest helicopter company in the world with vast resources, so it was easy for them to back deal with the farmer landlord. At my expense the newly formed Humber Airways (Ellerman Wilson) were also using Paull Aerodrome occasionally but not paying anything.

What should have been a pleasure, had the land been owned, was becoming a nightmare. Of my two sub-tenants, the impecunious Hull Aero Club could pay nothing, whilst Bristow Helicopters held out on paying. My lease with the farmer was rapidly becoming worthless. The banks would not loan money against a five-year planning term. With domestic problems at home, a young family and dwindling cash resources, I had to admit approaches to the city council in 1969 and the Lord Mayor in 1970 were unsuccessful, so there was no option but to withdraw my company's interest in the site.

238

An official memo from the East Yorkshire Aero Company Ltd:

"Old Vicarage
Bilton, Nr. Hull
HU11 4DZ
Tel. Hull 813393

A.N. Medforth (Managing)

Est. 1959

EAST YORKSHIRE AERO CO. LTD.

My company was formed in May 1959 for the express purpose of operating the pre-war municipal Aerodrome at Hedon to serve the City of Hull and environs. Unfortunately, an objection from a Saltend factory after the go-ahead had been given, produced a planning dispute between the local authorities. This eventually precluded the use of this excellent grass aerodrome although limited flying did take place in the 1959-61 period.

After a long search, an aerodrome was established on virgin farmland at Paull, a project which took four years to reach fruition. Here a complete absence of local authority support and banking assistance as well as leasing and planning restrictions prevented any reasonable sort of development taking place. Under such adverse conditions, my company was forced to relinquish options at Paull in 1970.

After a dormant spell it has been decided to renew activity in aviation. The lessons learned from the abortive projects at Hedon and Paull will stand the company in good stead for any future developments.

My company was formed in May 1959 for the express purpose of operating the pre-war municipal aerodrome at Hedon to serve the City of Hull and environs. Unfortunately, an objection from a Saltend factory after the go-ahead had been given produced a planning dispute between the local authorities. This eventually precluded the use of this excellent grass aerodrome although limited flying did take place in the 1959-61 period.

After a long search, an aerodrome was established on virgin farmland at Paull, a project which took four years to reach fruition. Here a complete absence of local authority support and banking assistance as well as leasing and planning restrictions prevented any reasonable sort of development taking place. Under such adverse conditions, my company was forced to relinquished options at Paull in 1970.

After a dormant spell it has been decided to renew activity in aviation. The lessons learned from the abortive projects at Hedon and Paull will stand the company in good stead for any future developments.

6.

The Beginning of the End

I was at the end of my tether and travelled down to London and Redhill, Surrey by train on the 19 March 1970. The idea was to try and save what was left of Paull Aerodrome, of my tenure; although isolated and having lost all my credibility, it was a last ditch attempt. I should have taken someone with me if only as a companion but as it was there was no one. Left with my thoughts for several hours and leaving behind me a shattered marriage, I was ill-prepared to face anyone, least of all representatives of the board of what was at that time, the largest helicopter company in the world.

How did I arrive in this position after only thirteen years before embarking on what I thought was the best option for me in the late fifties? Anyway, I arrived at Redhill in the early afternoon and the Bristow people took me out for a meal. They knew what they were on; I was plied with beer and wine. The meal was excellent and the alcohol was intoxicating. Already tired and worn out, I switched off and became half asleep, not even remembering my agenda. I was finished. On the way back from London I had sobered up and started to write up my notes on the train but it was too late… The turning point of my life had arrived.

Ellerman Wilson and their subsidiary Humber Airways closed down not long afterwards owing to the death of Sir John Ellerman. Bristow Helicopters continued at Paull until 1980 when a series of accidents contributed to the loss of their North Sea Oil BP contract. With them gone, poor Hull Aero Club could no longer pay the crippling rent to the farmer landlord who had put the squeeze on. It was a case of killing the goose that laid the golden egg.

In 1971, the land at Paull could be bought for £45,000, which would have made the difference. Ownership of the land or premises is essential, because the tender who are at the mercies of the landlords cannot be relied on. The concept or idea was there but the relatively small amount of capital needed was not. It is a great pity that the local authorities did not take more interest. In little more than ten years, I was back to square one from the Hedon go-ahead. Since then, there has been no sign of a local aerodrome for Hull, from the Hedon inquiry in January 1957, forty-nine years ago.

In 1980, it was the fiftieth anniversary of Amy Johnson's England to Australia flight which was celebrated at Paull as a joint venture between Hull Aero Club and the City Council. For some reason I did not receive an invite but such is life. Paull was used extensively, both by fixed wing aircraft and helicopters. In the absence of support from Hull Corporation which my company requested, the lease was given up. Hull Aero Club (which I helped to inaugurate) continued up until 1980 when crippling rental payments to the farmer landlord forced Paull's closure.

With some experience of helicopter operation gained at Paull, and having recovered somewhat from the Paull debacle, I decided to explore the possibility of setting up a Hull-based heliport. It would be around 1983 when I commenced negotiations with ABP who owned most if not all of the land fronting the River Humber – the old docklands taken over from the British Transport Docks Board after denationalisation. For reasons of safety, the Civil Aviation Authority will not allow helicopters to overfly built-up or residential areas.

7.

On Reflection

The 21st century is upon us. The millennium some prefer to call it. For me, it only marks one thing: that the city of Hull with a population of 300,000 still has not got its own airfield. This state of affairs must be without precedent in the British Isles seventy years ago, however this was not so. In fact in 1929, Hull was 'avant garde'. People were different and thought differently, everything was different – there was a brave new world to look forward to.

Billions of pounds are spent annually on bigger and better road systems for ever increasing numbers of cars. In the meantime, the city is continually overflown by a variety of aeroplanes but there is nowhere here for any of them to land. Any suggestion of 1,000 yards of tarmac being laid as an airstrip would doubtless be greeted with howls of protest from the authorities. Even the setting aside of a similar distance of grass strip would produce protests.

Bearing in mind the likely technical advances in the next century, with the certainty of short and vertical take-off being the vogue, provision for this must be made now. It seems to me therefore that any 21st century city plan must include 'local' air facilities within or near enough to the city to be effective for speedy air communication.

As I see it, there will be no local air facilities in the foreseeable future for the city of Hull and I stress that I do not refer to an international airport. The existence of Hedon Aerodrome was ignored for fifty years after World War II, apart from my occupation from 1958 to 1961. Furthermore, when the Hull Corporation ordered my company to leave in 1961, the backdoor to Hedon swung open and business light aircraft were landing quite frequently (see extract from Chamber of Commerce Report 1963).

Glancing through a recent copy of the Hull *Flashback* magazine, I came across some group photographs of Hull business and council representation, some of whom I had known more than forty years ago. Now for the first time, I became aware of something which had evaded me for years. I realised that I had little in common with these gentlemen.

Although younger, my early military training in the school Cadet Corps from 1937 and in the Home Guard from 1940, occupied all my spare time up to entering the army proper in 1943. After demob in late 1947, I finish up in the Reserve Army for ten years, following call up in 1951 when the Cold War with Russia started. I had worked for a Hull rivercraft company in the fifties and sixties following army service during and after the war. In spite of this, I could not match the experience of senior Hull businessmen and had the greatest respect for them. I should have been a part of them.

With hindsight and at the end of my life I will say this, life is so very short. As you grow from childhood through adolescence to maturity, there is a very limited period in which to seize on the few chances that occur in life. From day one you are dealt a hand of cards and the trick is to make the best of them.

On average, there are only ten or fifteen years when you are in your prime, and after that, arguably, you have missed the boat so to speak in some ways; I envy the present generation in being able to choose what they wish to do. In my father's day, and later mine, the two world wars took huge bites of time out of our lives and even survival without serious injury was not the only factor, as rebuilding post-war and settling down took time; yet we were still young men who wanted to fly – we were all young.

All these things happened a long time ago, back in the middle of the last century in fact. Most of the key people have passed on apart from myself, only a very few remain as witness to what went on. Of Napoleon, it was said that on his heart would be written 'Waterloo'. If this is possible then on my heart would be inscribed 'Hedon Aerodrome'.